What others are

"The story of Lanphier that Ken tells is made up of students who became future leaders who dot the landscape of this nation and, in particular, our local community. This work will highlight a particular place that remains a cornerstone of the Springfield we all know and love."—**Chuck Flamini**, former Lanphier Principal and School Board member and its past president.

"Author Ken Mitchell makes every attempt to amplify and recognize the history and personality of [Lanphier]. And that is the reason you will enjoy the stories about the many graduates and friends associated with what I call the 'Lion's Pride'." –**Art Spiegel** ('46), teacher and principal.

"If you have ever lived on the North End of Springfield, taught at Lanphier High School, or were ever an LHS student, you will relate to this terrific book so very well crafted by Ken Mitchell. It truly belongs in your personal library. You will find it a warm and inviting book that has been both intricately researched and lovingly presented."—**Raymond Bruzan**, Retired LHS chemistry teacher and Springfield Educator of the Year 1990.

"Mitchell has provided a fascinating insight into not only the beginnings of Lanphier High School but a very candid look at the tremendous issues that faced educators, students and parents in the '60s, '70s and '80s." –**Robert "Bob" C. Lanphier III**, grandson of the co-founder of Sangamo Electric and former president and CEO of DICKEY-John.

"Once I started it, I couldn't put it down. I really loved it. I don't read many books these days... but this one I had to read."—**Ossie Langfelder** *('44) and former Mayor of Springfield.*

"My wife Gloria and I have lived in the North End our entire lives. People often ask, 'What is meant by the words, I AM PROUD TO BE A NORTH ENDER?' If you have not lived here, you would not understand. Ken has done an outstanding job explaining why he is proud to be a North Ender. This book is a <u>must read</u> for those interested in the history of the North End and Lanphier High School." –**Bob Nika** ('55), Lanphier basketball player, teacher and basketball coach of the 1983 State Championship team.

"Ken Mitchell has done a remarkably thorough job in writing this book. The story of Lanphier High School and Springfield's North End comes alive through dozens of interviews, historical research, and archival photos. Every Lanphier graduate should have this book as a reminder of the school's heritage."—**Virginia Scott**, former Executive Director, Illinois Environmental Council.

"What a wonderful read. I enjoyed so much reading about my alma mater. There's a lot of interesting information in those pages, not only about Lanphier, but also about the surrounding area. The many pictures in the book help to show what words cannot convey. It brought back a lot of old memories. My mom and dad used to brag a lot about Reservoir Park. Now I know why." –**Jerry Tansky** (Class of '59), Customer and Quality Control Manager.

"Lanphier was more than a school—it taught us about life." **—Phil Martin** (Class of '49), former Art teacher in Taylorville and substitute teacher in District #186.

"I came to Lanphier in '43... I really enjoyed the school and the people. They let me do what I knew how to do in photography. It was a real difference: they were more my kind of people at Lanphier."—**Dave Beatty** (Class of '46), Professional photographer.

"Ken Mitchell has gathered the 77-year history of Lanphier High School...and brought it to life in his book. North-End Pride *is well written, interacts how world, national, and city developments affected changes in the personality and character of LHS throughout the years. It is a MUST READ because it gets to the heart and soul of the people of LHS and Springfield. I know because I have directly been a part of Lanphier for the last 47 years."* **—Steve Rambach,** Lanphier's longest-serving teacher.

"It's an impressive accomplishment! ... I enjoyed reading it. "**—Alice Armstrong**, District #186 high school English teacher.

"Once again Ken Mitchell gives his readers a glimpse of what life was like on Springfield's North End. The fascinating story of Lanphier High School comes alive with accounts of its beginnings and subsequent history told by the author with the help of others" --**Curtis Mann**, *Manager, Sangamon Valley Collection.*

North-End Pride:

The Story of Lanphier High School,

Its People and Community

By

Kenneth C. Mitchell

 **Seagull Press**

North-End Pride: The Story of Lanphier High School, Its People and Community
By Kenneth C. Mitchell

ISBN 978-1-4951-3211-7

A grateful acknowledgement to the following sources for allowing their pictures, drawings, and parts of articles to be reproduced in this book: *State Journal-Register*; the *Jacksonville Journal Courier*; Nick Johnson, Peoria Astronomical Society; and William Crook, Jr. , local artist.

Seagull Press Publishing Company
Post Office Box 9345
Springfield, IL 62791-9345
(217) 787-7100
www.KenMitchellBooks.com

Printed in the United States of America
By Faith Printing
824 Bills Rd., Franklin, IL 62638
Phone 217.675.2191
www.faithprinting.net

Eight Printing: March 2019

10 9 8 7
Covers by Dolce Design
Tony Sanguedolce
email: antoniodd2@yahoo.com
website: http://sanguedolcedesign.wordpress.com/portfolio/

LANPHIER

HIGH SCHOOL

Other Works by Ken Mitchell

Books

Rabbit Row: The Life and Times of J.P. Mitchell, KM&A Press, Springfield, IL, 2004, 372 pages

Sister Raphael: The Personal and Family History of Jennie Roscetti Mitchell, KM&A Publishing, Springfield, IL, 2006, 290 pages

In the Bonds: Fraternity Life in the '60s, Seagull Press, Springfield, IL, 2009, 352 pages

Shorter Works

"The Child of Your Dreams," Chapter 13, *Jose Silva's UltraMind ESP System,* Career Press, Franklin Lakes, NJ, edited by Ed Bernd, Jr., 2001

Leaving Your Legacy: How to Record Your Personal Story or Family History, KM&A Press, 2008, 38 pages. (This is the workbook for his seminar "Writing Your Own Life Story.")

My Friend Bunk: Hubert A. "Bunk" Douglas, KM&A Publishing, Springfield, IL, 2009, 58 pages

Converse Kids: A Memoir on Growing Up, Seagull Press, Springfield, IL, 2009, 41 pages

At the Top of My Game: My Five Years in the Life Insurance Business, Seagull Press, Springfield, IL, 2011, 105 pages

My Fantastic Vision, Seagull Press, 2000, 6 pages

Law School Days, Seagull Press, 2013, 13 pages

I'm in the Army Now, Seagull Press, 2013, 34 pages

Summer Vacation 1980, Seagull Press, 2013, 11 pages

Edited Works

The Life and Times of Hugo Antonacci, Hugo Antonacci, Springfield, IL, December 1998, 145 pages.

The Curse of the Unpardonable Sin: My Struggles from Underdevelopment and My Emergence from Darkness, David E. Johnson, Springfield, IL, 2009

Dedication

Eugene "Gene" Stevenson

1930-1946

Gene passed away while saving a fellow Lanphier student and friend in a boating accident.

This Plaque is in the front lobby of LHS

The front entrance of Lanphier High School, facing Eleventh
Street. [1989 *Lan-Hi*]

Contents

Robert C. Lanphier [Courtesy of Robert C. Lanphier III]

Foreword

Ken Mitchell has brought alive the very meaning of a 'North Ender,' as he depicts the origins and life of Lanphier High School. From relating the roots of the people that made up the 'North Enders,' he describes their love for their Reservoir Park and how their park was handed over to the Springfield School Board, where it became the grounds for a new high school and sports stadium.

This book is more than just a factual history of the times and events of these happenings. Mitchell also brings out what made 'North Enders' the fine people that lived in the northeast part of Springfield...their ethics, their morality, their work standards, their loyalty, their feeling for their community, their devotion to their neighbors, and their dedication to their neighborhood.

Mitchell has provided a fascinating insight into not only the beginnings of Lanphier High School but a very candid look at the tremendous issues that faced educators, students and parents in the '60s,'70s and '80s. This was an incredible period of cultural change, as issues dealing with overcrowding, bussing, gender equality, race relations and technological improvements created very real dilemmas for administrators, students, parents, and their community.

I heard my father (Robert C. Lanphier, Jr.) speak warmly of 'North Enders' at our dinner table, and I was privileged to work with them during my ten years at Sangamo, where my last office looked out directly on Lanphier High School. Best of all, in 1995 I married a

"North Ender," and Lanphier High School graduate, Phylliss Catron, class of '55.

My first employment at Sangamo was in the summers of 1952 and 1953 in the incomparable Tool and Die Department, working with around 110 tool and die journeymen under General Foreman Ben Rodrick. I had firsthand experience working with some of the finest men I have ever known, virtually all 'North Enders'…not that during coffee breaks they didn't secretly substitute a rubber bit in my shaping machine, or glue a large screw to my brand new Craftsman toolbox to make it look like it went right through the corner…good fun. Those men made the dies, the fixtures and the tools that produced the parts for all Sangamo products, and they kept all of the equipment working: the molding machines, the screw machines, the punch presses, and everything else required to manufacture and assemble the precision products Sangamo built.

Recently, I read the book *Boys in the Boat* by Daniel James Brown, the story of nine untrained young men who through determination and grit went on to win the 1936 eight-man crew race in Berlin. Brown's story of the boys is spellbinding, but he also weaves in the horrors of the depression and of the dust bowl, as well as describing the facade created by Hitler to impress other countries. Ken Mitchell similarly weaves into the story of Lanphier High School the social and cultural changes of those times and how the people at Lanphier addressed those challenges, mostly with incredible success.

Mitchell has produced a document that will forever describe one of the most challenging times of our community and of our past.

Robert Carr Lanphier III
Glen Arbor, Michigan
October 8, 2014

Robert "Bob" C. Lanphier III, grandson of Sangamo's co-founder Robert C. Lanphier, Sr., followed in his father's and grandfather's footsteps, graduating from Yale with an electrical engineering degree. He worked at Sangamo Electric Company for 10 years, leaving as assistant vice president and manager of its communications division. He worked for DICKEY-john Corp. for 21 years as manager, president, and then chairman of the board. He founded AGMED Corp. and was its president for 15 years prior to what has been an active retirement. He has been in a number of professional organizations, including the National Academy of Engineering; chairman of the Farm and Industrial Equipment Institute; and president of the American Society of Agricultural Engineers. He spent 28 years with the Memorial Medical System, as a director and later chairman.

Memories & Futures

Toward the beginning of the movie *Dead Poets Society*, the beloved boys prep school English teacher, Mr. Keating (played by the late Robin Williams), brings his class out into the hall to instruct them on yet another life lesson. He asks them to view the old display case in the hall that every student passes several times a day and yet never "sees." We have those display cases at Lanphier too, with awards and trophies and pictures of long-gone graduated boys and girls. He begins his lesson with the words from Robert Herrick's poem "To the Virgins, to Make Much of Time":

> *"Gather ye rose buds while ye may,*
> *Old time is still a flying.*
> *And this same flower that smiles today*
> *Tomorrow will be dying."*

After Mr. Keating explains that those young, vital-looking athletes are now long dead—like the roses in the poem— he asks his class that essential question we must all ask of ourselves, "Did they wait til it was too late to make from their lives even one iota of what they were capable?"

He then finishes this important scene with a charge to his students: *"Carpe diem...carpe diem...*seize the day, boys. Make your lives extraordinary."

As Mr. Keating opens his students' eyes and hearts to his advice, perhaps you, the reader, will take time to do the same. Like the present day Lanphier students, you too still have time to make your life extraordinary.

Preface

This is not the story of a 150,000-square-foot building with halls and rooms that was our city's third high school. Nor is it the 10-square-mile piece of land called the North End. This is the story of people.

People who bought and worked this land. People who labored in the mines and factories and built the community and had children. And people who built the park that gave those children recreation. And the people who cried out when that park was torn down for that new high school. People who built the school, and people who have administered and taught the 40,000 kids who have attended the school. And those kids who became contributing members of the community and the larger society.

It's also about the man who gave the school its name. He wasn't just a community leader and the head of the factory across the street from the school. He was a family man who sometimes made pottery. He was an adventurer and a good guy who gave money to the hospital and to other worthy causes. He did all these things while battling cancer for many years without so much as a whimper. This book is about all these people.

The idea for it sprang from a draft I wrote for another book. A couple of years ago I decided to pen a memoir about my time at Lanphier High School in Springfield, Illinois. It was to be published in time for our 1962 50th Class Reunion. When that didn't materialize, I laid the draft down to finish it "someday."

A few months ago I'd thought I better put on the final touches of the memoir with the working title *Happy Times at Lanphier High: Memoir of the Class of '62*. After reading it over I felt that I should include two or three pages about the history of our school, to give the book some context about where LHS came from.

Lo and behold, by mid-summer I was already into page 50 of the history, and I wasn't done yet. With more interviews to conduct and more research to gather, I thought to myself, *Why not write this as a book to stand on its own?* And so it is. It's a rather short book, but filled with lots of pictures which tell the story in their own way.

Since I am substitute teaching and much of it at Lanphier, I am hoping Lanphier students will enjoy knowing about their school's history. If they will have it, I will see if we can eventually dedicate a small corner of the school library for a display case of Lanphier memorabilia to go along with the seventy-seven-year history this book contains.

I am also hoping that all North Enders—native sons and daughters as well as those other Springfieldians with the North-End spirit and pride—will embrace this book as an appreciation of our upbringing on the north side of "Springpatch."

In researching the Lanphier history, I discovered there was no place one could go to find anywhere near a comprehensive look at how our high school came to be, not any but the briefest historical sketches. The best were from a couple of *Lan-Hi* anniversary issues. So as far as I know, this is the only history book on Lanphier High School. Here's hoping you will find it interesting and enlightening.

Kenneth C. Mitchell
November 1, 2014

"In Praise of North Enders"
By Ken Mitchell

- They talk plainly with unvarnished words.
- They call it as it is, so you always know where they stand.
- They pay their own way and give charity to others.
- They put in an honest day's work and expect others to do the same.
- They take pride in doing things the right way.
- They finish what they start.
- They believe their best days are ahead of them.
- They expect their children will have a better life than they've had.
- They believe in God and aren't afraid to say so.
- They will do what it takes to protect their families.
- They respect their houses, yards, and neighborhoods.
- They love their country and its flag.
- Their word is their bond.
- They take their vote seriously and tell others to do the same.
- They obey the laws even when others aren't around.
- They are honest in dealing with others.
- They believe in sportsmanship and that winning isn't the only thing.

Acknowledgements

I want to thank the following people for their help in making this book possible.

The staff at the Sangamon Valley Collection of the Springfield Lincoln Library: Curtis Mann, manager, Beth Shetter and Linda Garvert; and Tom Fitch, a volunteer at the SVC, who spent years writing the statistics on all Springfield boys' basketball teams onto a CD.

To the following alumni and others who took time for interviews, articles, and helped me with facts:

Former students: Celia Antonacci-Frasco Ackerman ('37); Dave Beard ('53); Dave Beatty ('46); Randy Blair ('78); Dorothy Boehner ('43); Dave Dalbey ('58); Helen Noll Deverman ('64); Phil Irving ('75); Charliene Tucker Kloppenburg ('45); Henry "Bud" Kloppenburg ('44); Gary Kreppert ('55); Donna Cornish Krueger ('46); Ossie Langfelder ('44); Phil Martin ('49); Randy Miller ('71); Bob Nika ('55); Phil Shadid ('57); Art Spiegel ('46); Jerry Tansky ('59); Beccie Tygett ('62); Bill Utterback ('55); Sandy Mitchell Utterback ('58).

Former and current teachers: Carl Birkner; Ray Bruzan; Jim Gardner; Marilyn Gardner; Lee Halberg; Helen Bellamy Holm; Deb Huffman; Betsy Lair; Arlyn Lober; Cindy Luton; Don Post; Steve Rambach; and Mark Scheffler.

Other contributors: Nancy Lanphier Chapin; Marcia Bullard; Eileen Bullard; Jim Ruppert; Charlie Schweighauser; Larry Davsko; Howard Hoehn; John Kohlrus, Paul Palazzolo; Rich Saal; William Crook, Jr.; Farrell Gay; and Andrew Call.

To the *Lan-Hi* staff, its advisors, Brendon Thompson and Jennifer Vargas, and Katie Fitzgerald for taking pictures; to Cassidy Johnson from Photography class for taking pictures; to Barb Volkman, Lanphier Hall of Fame advisor; and Monique Davis, Lanphier school newspaper advisor.

To our fine group of eagle-eye reviewers: Alice Armstrong; Katie Fitzgerald ('15); Karen Kelly; Charliene Tucker Kloppenburg ('45); Curtis Mann; Steve Rambach; Virginia Scott and Jerry Tansky ('59).

To Principal Chuck Flamini and Principal Larry Rowe, for giving me insight into Lanphier during their tenures.

To all those unsung heroes and heroines, over the years, responsible for having made Lanphier run smoother: teachers, spouses of teachers, administrative staff, custodians, tradesmen, contractors, food services personnel, and security detail. Thank you for all your hard work— many times under adverse circumstances.

A special appreciation to Bob Lanphier for his encouragement, information on the Watch Factory and Sangamo Electric, family pictures, and insight into his grandfather's personal life.

To my family for their forbearance during the many months of time I spent in my study: my wonderful wife, Karen Kelly, an exemplary teacher in her own right; our outstanding daughter, Zemfira; and our family best friend, "Annie," who would sit by me as I typed away, laying her head on my leg, with her sad eyes looking up at me, as if to say, "Please, take me out now."

To Brad Books from Capitol Blue Print, Inc. for all of his work with page design and the printing process. He spent a lot of time fixing my spacing and re-edits, a time-consuming proofing process.

Although my reviewers did a fine job, it's finally up to me to make sure I got rid of all the typos, misspellings, plus grammar and sentence errors. If any of you readers find them floating around, please bring them to my attention. And most importantly, if I missed any of Lanphier's other main events, remarkable teachers or standout athletes, I am sorry. Send me those things and people I missed and I'll try to put them in subsequent printings, where practical.

Introduction

When I began attending Lanphier High School it was relatively new—just 22 years old—having opened its doors on January 25, 1937. Everyone in the North End of Springfield was excited by the news of a brand new high school that all the area kids could attend. Just a generation before, many children did not attend school beyond the eighth grade.

My father was one of those unfortunate children whose life, he thought, was diminished by that limitation. Stopping after eighth grade in 1922 was a regret of his I heard many times. When he worked at the Watch Factory, none other than Mr. Bunn, its president, offered to pay for his engineering training if he would go to high school, but Dad's vision was scarred by a difficult upbringing where education was not even on his parents' radar.

Then there was a young Italian North-End boy who wanted to attend high school in the worst way but couldn't in the normal timeframe because he had to work and help support his family during the late '20s and into the Depression years. Paul LaFata lived close to the future Lanphier, on Pennsylvania Avenue, and worked for a druggist from ages 14 through 20. He talks about *his* vision in his revealing autobiography, *My Story: Determination, Hard Work and Faith*:

> It was while working as an apprentice pharmacist that I decided to become a doctor rather than a pharmacist. I recalled my eighth-grade teacher (a nun) telling us on graduation to "aim high" when selecting a

vocation. So I took the high aim toward medicine. I must have been very naïve not to consider lack of high school as a deterrent to higher education. At any rate, I decided to skip high school and in 1932... [entered] Springfield College....

By the thirties, most parents wanted their children to attend high school, and those on the North End were excited about the possibility of a new school making it easier for them to do so. (Mom had to navigate the three miles from her 19th and Converse home all the way to Central High and then Springfield High.) But even in light of this anticipation for a new high school, its planning, construction and opening were marred by a controversy over its location. It was to be situated at the west end of what had been Reservoir Park, a beautiful and revered 24-acre green oasis in Springfield, where the North-End citizens enjoyed weekdays and weekends, summer boating and winter skating, for seventy-five years.

Before we get deeper into that contentious beginning, I will lay out what it was like growing up as a North Ender, next a brief history of the Springfield school system, then Lanphier's place in it. The North-End employers allowed its citizens to earn decent livelihoods, so we will explore their place in the development of this side of Springfield. In the rest of the book, I will summarize some of Lanphier's major events and people throughout its history, through the nine decades of its memorable existence.

The Lanphier High School ring was available to its students from the inception of the school. [1949 *Lan-Hi*]

Street view of the Pantheon, from in front of Coutrakon's. Watt Brothers Pharmacy had moved from next to the theater to the SW corner of 9th and North Grand (see sign). From the movie titles and the parked Chevy, it was 1961. [Courtesy of Sangamon County Tax Assessor Office]

Chapter 1

The North End

I wasn't born on the north side of Springfield but I was raised as a North Ender from age three on. I spent all my formative years there and am proud to call myself by that name. I am a North Ender through and through.

We came to Springfield from Cicero, just west of Chicago. I was actually born a few blocks inside the city, at Garfield Park Hospital, but our apartment was in Cicero, where my sister Sandy and I lived for two years. My mom and dad were both raised on the North End, about a mile away from each other, but never knew one another. Ironically, they met in Chicago, just a year or so after Mom had left the Franciscan Order as a pediatric nurse.

With the financial help of my grandfather, they built a small frame house at 1719 East Converse, east of Lanphier a few blocks, in 1947. When I say small, I mean small: two tiny bedrooms, a hallway, a kitchen and a bath. The basement was dug out a couple of years after we moved in. Dad proudly would talk about our house having "all Grade-A lumber" in it, something that was lost on me until years later. I remember Dad and his Italian brothers-in-law nail on those common gray Transite shingles as siding and then pave the driveway with cinders. We didn't have a garage for several years. Some of our neighbors built their houses the other way around. They dug a basement first and lived in it a few years until they could afford the top half. Flat houses with tarpaper protecting their tops, with characteristic staircases jutting out of them were not all that uncommon on the North End in the late forties.

Almost all North Enders had vegetable gardens in their back yards. Mom was the steward of ours, and Sandy and I got to weed it all summer long. Our garden also served as our pet cemetery. Some future owner of our house will find, among others, our dog Dagwood and my pet bird in a sealed Ball jar some day and wonder their origin. We supplemented our home-grown food by hunting berries near Andrew (ten miles north of Springfield), where Dad fished at Brown's Pond for crappie and bass and an occasional snapping turtle. He sure loved turtle soup; the name and main ingredient repulsed me.

Each spring we had a ritual of foraging dandelion greens on the Illinois State Fair grounds. They looked and tasted like endive, but were free for the taking. Friends wrinkle their noses when I mention eating them, but they should read Rebecca Wood's blog which calls dandelion leaves "the most nutritious leafy vegetable you can buy," so I guess our parents knew what they were doing: Dad lived to 87 and Mom to 102. Sandy and I would assist Mom canning dozens of jars of fruit and veggies. Mom also killed chickens in our basement every couple of weeks. I grew up knowing personally what the phrase "running around like a chicken with its head cut off" meant. I can still smell those boiled feathers. Except for Dad, we accepted the Italian delicacy of gnawing on chicken feet in our pasta. I considered myself more Italian than English—"Johnnie Bull," my grandparents would disparagingly refer to my English heritage— because of my affinity for Italian food and visiting my grandparents daily.

That home and that neighborhood, smack in the middle of the North End, defined my youth and my values. I would like to share with you some of my background growing up because it will give you a sense of what Lanphier students—North-End Kids— were made of, and, to a degree, still are. (Much of the following references are from my short memoir, *Converse Kids: A Memoir on Growing Up*.)

Most all of my memories of my childhood are unabashedly happy ones, even though we had no money to speak of. I can't imagine a better neighborhood to grow up in or a better time. I was one of a couple of dozen kids on or near Converse Avenue in Springfield in the 1950s. And from the ages of seven to fourteen, I was inseparable from them; we were practically family. We took care of the younger kids, and we were watched over by the older ones.

We changed sports with each season; we adventured around our world at will on our trusty used bikes; we bought baseball cards by recycling pop bottles at two cents each; we experimented with all kinds of fun hobbies; and we seemed to laugh our way through childhood, abiding by the injunction, "Don't worry—be happy!" Both Dave Johnson and Lennie Kunz, fellow "Converse Kids," told me at a recent reunion that they worried about such things as the atom bomb and communism. Fortunately I was oblivious to current events, and saved myself that angst. Still, we had an exhilarating optimism about our futures.

There were four unwritten rules sacred to us all: baseball was king; fighting was avoided; girls were not allowed to play with us; and we honored all those 12 Boy Scout rules without even knowing about their existence until we joined up. In a word, we were all good kids and our parents were happy to have us. It was so close to Garrison Keillor's Lake Wobegon credo it was scary: "Where all the women are strong, all the men are good looking, and all the children are above average."

At the risk of sounding corny, many people on the North End in those days could be considered the salt of the earth. They were Middle America writ large. One of the most poignant descriptions of the average people in our small part of this world is summed up by our grocer, Johnnie Kohlrus, in his memoir *Family*, when he talks about his parents:

> My mother and father were a tribute to the human race, as most people were back in those days. They were honest, their word was as good as gold, and they worked—and worked hard, not only my mom and dad, but the whole family….

Part of my idyllic childhood was luck: the war was over, prosperity and confidence in the "American Way" were at a high, and we were able to grow into adolescence without fear. We were insulated from outside insults. Of course, no one on our block had much money: all our parents were lower middle class—very low in some cases. Our parents even pooled their old clothing to help a couple of families who were, as my dad described them, as poor as Job's turkey. There were only two men on my block who were not blue-collar: Mr. Alvin Hahn, a minister who taught at the nearby Lutheran grade school, and Mr. Larry Delaney who worked as a manager at Sangamo. I was impressed, and a bit confused, seeing them go to work wearing suits and ties.

The other part of our good fortune was that our parents were one hundred percent committed to our growing up "better than we had it". That was just one of the Great Depression phrases that taught us that we were being protected from what our parents had to endure during their growing-up years. They figured the best way to do that was a solid education—and the more education, the better. I can only think of a few neighborhood kids who did not eventually attend college, so our parents did a good job fulfilling their wish for a better life for us.

The street boundaries of our childhood world ran pretty much with the four railroad tracks that closed us in and kept us safe: Watch Avenue on the north (B&O railroad), Wheeler Avenue on the east (B&O spur), North Grand Avenue on the south (Wabash railroad) and Michigan Avenue on the west (C&IM railroad).

Speaking of railroads, we also had to contend with trains stopping for long periods of time at 15th and Converse. We grew up with the last of the hulky steam locomotives with their piercing whistles belching up black plumes of smoke as they carried long lines of coal cars through our neighborhood to power plants in Chicago.

Those 15 or so blocks of protected territory were plenty of room for us to play and learn for the first several years of our lives. We eventually expanded our world as maturity and bravery allowed us, to explore as far as our bikes would take us, within reason. Even during our adventurous years, if we strayed too far from home or were seen too late in the evening, some conscientious neighbor would stop what he was doing in his front yard and say, "Hey, aren't you that Mitchell kid? ...You better get the hell home or I'll call your parents! Now get home, right now!" That was both reassuring to us (everybody seemed to care about us) and disappointing (we were in fact on a very short leash).

That was the neighborhood I remember and cherish. The one thing I can't remember, however, is how I got from my grandparents' garage-house when we first moved to town to discover the kids who would become my playmates for the next several years. All I recall is that we built our house on Converse and, voila, the other kids just appeared, all fully formed and ready for friendship. Dave Johnson recently told me he first remembered meeting me when we were five or six, at the play area in Lincoln Park, where our parents chatted as we played.

One difference among us kids was schools: about half went to the public school, which was Bunn, and the rest of us were Catholics and attended St. Aloysius. I was always envious of my Protestant friends because they seemed to have more fun at Bunn. They probably felt the same about us at St. Al's, except for having to attend Mass every single day—yuk, who would have wanted that? We never had time or inclination to talk about religion, though: we were too busy thinking of fun things to do after school—and all during those luscious summer days when we habitually carried salt shakers for tomatoes and green apples. Dave Johnson admitted to me recently that his minister referred to Catholicism as that "great whore of Babylon," something, if he had told me that back then, would have confused me to no end.

Many of my friends at Lanphier attended Third Pres church, which was ruled over by long-time minister, Rev. H. M. Hildebrandt. Hero and icon of North-End Presbyterians, Rev. Hildebrandt had that ministry for more than 50 years. He was in fact my father's minister when he was a boy. My dad spoke affectionately about him many times. He told me the reverend never owned a car but would visit parishioners on foot all those years. When I was a teen, Jay Gobble and family were Third Pres members and stayed so until they moved out of state in his early 30s. At its height Third Pres had over 3,400 members.

Reverend Hildebrandt's North-End counterpart in the Catholic Church was "Father Al," our priest at St. Aloysius. Monsignor Bertman, his official name, came to St. Al's when our new church was dedicated in 1955. An autocratic leader with a booming voice, Father Al made sure his parish ran smoothly. He was also a principal fundraiser for Fairview Park, a North-End recreational spot at Griffiths and 19th Street.

North Enders have always been hard-working, patriotic, fun loving, and fiercely devoted to their families. Here's how a newspaper characterized them:

> "North enders" describes a community of individuals bonded together by an awareness of their past and by a sense of belonging. They have always had a solid sense of who they are and why they are here.

When we kids were ready to play Little League ball, Father Al, Ed Vespa, Bill Cellini, Sr., and a dozen other neighbors decided to build a park, and they did it. Through ingenuity and industriousness, they formed the Fairview Improvement Association. They raised money by going door to door and got the job done in record time to allow us to play Little League, PONY League, and enjoy Saturday night under-the-stars movies at Fairview Park. Every time I pass by that park today, I can see, through the mists of time, Bill Cellini, Sr., Vic Gent, my dad and others readying our ball diamond and having fun in the process. Dad also plumbed the concession stand and toilets. There is a plaque there today dedicated to those men and women who made that little park possible. Those were North Enders.

There were a lot of Italian and German families in and around the North End. When I went to St. Al's, many of my classmates were from Devereux Heights, a small hamlet north of Sangamon Avenue, with around 30 families. Most of them were Italians, and according to my second-grade teacher, Sister Louise (Gietl), "Most were a rough group of boys, I can tell you that. My fellow sisters from other schools used to feel sorry for us." Most of the Italian kids graduated to Cathedral or Ursuline, but many, like me, elected to attend Lanphier. (Some of the Ursuline girls came over to Lanphier after their first year. My sister was one of them.) All the Lutheran kids went to Lanphier because there was no Lutheran high school in town.

In the late '40s household pantries and ice boxes were filled weekly by the wives who shopped at the many corner grocery stores. Johnie Kohlrus told me that there were 350 such neighborhood grocery stores dotting Springfield's landscape before supermarkets like Piggly-Wiggly and National came in. My Uncle Harley and Aunt Viola ran Mitchell's Market in Oak Knolls –Dad calling that area the high- rent district— for many years until the big grocery chains displaced him and his other Independent Grocery Association store partners, whom he helped organize under the IGA banner.

Harley began his climb to prosperity out of the North End by apprenticing at Freddie Noll's grocery store, just a block south of Lanphier on a small wedge of property squeezed between 13th and Reservoir and the railroad tracks. A small clutch of students would run to Noll's at lunch and get sandwiches or tamales and soda pops until the school district closed all public high school campuses. Our neighborhood stores were Mack's and Kohlrus's and Brook's. Mom only used Tony Brook's if we needed something in a rush.

The other neighborhood staples were taverns. They were about as commonplace as grocery stores. They seemed to be on every corner where grocery stores were not. Converse and 16th had a tavern (Russ Richards') but the two I was most familiar with were on 19th and Cummins (Viola's) and Mary's Friendly Tavern a few doors down on 19th and North Grand. The Italians and Germans would be seen in both, after a back breaking day at the mines. My bachelor uncle, Percy Roscetti, also a coal miner, frequented Viola's. It had a bocce ball court right behind it, close to the tracks.

My friends and I grew up watching old Italian men while away their afternoons by rolling those small bocce balls down the dirt courts. They never tired of that game. My friend Louis Marcie reminded me recently that some of the kids would tease the old men when they had too much to drink by running up and taking balls off the court.

Many a hot summer evening Uncle Percy would walk over to our house carrying a jug of beer (and gnawing on a cigar) to share it with Dad as they would listen to ball games and shoot the breeze. Mom, Sandy and I would join them on our porch drinking sugary lemonade. That is one of my most comforting childhood memories.

Like most families in those days, the man of the house worked a job and the little lady stayed in the house as a "homemaker." Dad was in the Plumbers and Steamfitters Union, Local #137. He was a certified welder, a rare distinction back then which made him more valuable. Still though, he worked at the behest of the BA, or business agent, Charlie Carey, who would call Dad when jobs became available. Most winters he was out of work for several weeks which made our belt tightening very uncomfortable.

Some men worked in the many area coal mines and at the two principal North-End industries, the Sangamo Electric Company (earlier the Illinois Watch Company) and Pillsbury Mills. Sangamo and the Mill employed over 2,000 workers. Other business enterprises dotted these neighborhoods as well, such as the C&IM railroad yard next to the Mill, the Paint Factory, and the International Shoe Company. (The shoe factory employed several hundred workers, mainly women in low-paying jobs. But, they were jobs.)

Most of our neighbors made similar wages, no matter where they worked. We knew we were toward the bottom of the economic heap, just like we knew families whose kids went to Springfield High were considerably above us, sometimes very much above us. We never took a vacation and I don't recall once going out to a restaurant when I was growing up. Mom and Dad went to The Mill Restaurant on North 15th Street a couple of times when he worked for plumbing contractor Artie Weiskoft who put on a Christmas party for his employees. But that was our lot and the only thing we could do was work hard in school to climb our way into the middle of the middle class someday.

Lanphier Neighborhoods

I wasn't in a neighborhood that had a nickname, but many of them that feed into the Lanphier district did. There was Starnes with its mainly Italian families just north of Grandview. Another Italian community, Little Italy, was around where Concordia Seminary was later built: 15th and Moffat Streets. Mill Row took its name from the Springfield Rolling Mill, which was one of the first major factories (of steel rails) that helped develop the North End into the city's industrial base. Its neighborhood was North 14th Street between the 1700 and 1800 blocks.

The name "Ridgely" had been used to loosely describe a general area all the way from Rabbit Row north to the Fair Grounds. It originated, however, as a definite place, the Village of Ridgely, which was south and east of the Fair Grounds, and annexed into the city in 1883. At the same time it was incorporated, the Village of North Springfield failed to receive enough votes to come in. Lying south of Ridgely, North Springfield eventually was included, and those two territories (much of which had been owned as farm ground by Henry Converse) comprise a lot of what we call the North End.

Then there was the Hay Homes development on 11th Street just north of Madison. It was a public housing project that served post-war families who were saving up to buy a house. When I was in school the Hay Homes was in the process of changing into a nearly all black community. There had also been a black neighborhood north of the Hay Homes around the Palmer school location.

The Enos Park area, south of the North Grand Avenue business district and down to Carpenter Street, was also a fairly distinct community. Its social hub was Third Presbyterian church, and next to it was Enos Park itself. Today the Enos Park district is being transformed back into the same kind of working class area it had been for nearly a century, thanks to the Enos Park Neighborhood Association, one of the most active in the city.

I don't know if they considered themselves in Enos Park—they were—or gave themselves their own neighborhood name, but Springfield Lithuanians had a vibrant cultural oasis north of Carpenter and west of 9th Street for many, many years. Their community touchstone was St. Vincent de Paul church and school. Church services were conducted in their own language by Father Yunkers, a force of a man with lots of hobbies and interests. I used to ask my dad to drive past their church on Eighth and Enos Streets to look at his big telescope sticking out of an observatory he built next to the rectory.

Little Italy was a concentration of Italian families close to Concordia Seminary. It was generally inside the area bounded by Reynolds, Fiftheenth, Carpenter, and Eighth Streets. The hub of it was Sgro's Grocery Store on 11th and Enos. Here's how Sam A. Sgro described how neighborhood grocery stores contributed even more than food to their communities. This is from his memorable oral history interview in 1972. [See Works Cited in the back of this book.]:

> They were actually centers for activity in each neighborhood. Gossip was passed and food prepared and so forth...Our store, or my grandfather's store at the time, was a center for the Italian-speaking people who couldn't use the English language too well. My grandfather was one of the fortunate ones who knew how to read and write in Italian and in English. Consequently his store served as a clearing house for most of the business transacted in the neighborhood, not only in food, but legal documents and so forth.

What I will call the Fairview neighborhood was and is a vibrant neighborhood from north of Sangamon Avenue down to Black Avenue and west to 14th Street and east through Northgate. Just north of Sangamon Avenue was Devereux Heights neighborhood, a small and tightknit group of families. While many of them were Catholic and probably went to Cathedral and Ursuline, others I knew gravitated to Lanphier.

There were other interesting communities around the North End like Goosetown and Dog Patch and Sand Hill.

Goosetown was a mostly German community on the southwest edge of the North End, near where the Memorial Medical Center is today. It was centered around the Old Reisch Brewery, which provided incomes for over 50 families. Begun in 1849 and closing in 1966, Reisch Brewery and its family members comprise an amazing Springfield story in its own right, fit for a book. The neighborhood was actually home to two other breweries during the early years—Kuykendall's Brewery and Ackerman's Brewery.

The last neighborhood I will describe is Hollywood. Lying west of MacArthur and north of Jefferson, its 20 or so blocks held the most interest to me as I grew up. For some reason my dad knew the area well and would take me through it. I had the feeling that I was somehow trespassing and entering an area I may not be able to get out of. It is still a mystery to many Springfield residents and unknown to others. It was the most economically depressed neighborhood in town, with some homes having only two rooms. It had more than its share of basement houses. A 1947 county judge is reputed to have commented about its youth that "the majority of juvenile delinquency in Sangamon County occurs in Hollywood."

I always thought of our North End as a distinct land unto itself. There is an esprit de corps that permeates all North Enders. Journalist Judy Miller caught its flavor in a newspaper article when she said, "The North End of

Springfield is a lot like an old pair of shoes. A little scruffy, but such a comfortable fit that the wearer hates to change."

Many North Enders never do change, their addresses that is. They have that innate North- End pride and stay planted. They may move into updated subdivisions like Northgate or Indian Hills or Twin Lakes (or even Sherman), but they stay North Enders nonetheless. When I moved back home from living in a small farm town and bought a house on the west side, my mother had a fit. "Why didn't you come back to the North End?" she asked with a sincere sadness and puzzlement. I didn't have a ready answer and still don't.

Bob Lanphier and I had lunch one day when he brought up a point that I had not considered as I wrote this book. He observed that the North End is the only part of Springfield that has its own distinct identity: "The West Side doesn't have it, neither does the South or East in the same emotional way. In a sense it is more a state of mind than a place." When was the last time you saw someone wearing a T-Shirt bragging about where they lived? Only when a North Ender was wearing one.

Fred Noll Groceries & Meats at 13th and Reservoir St. Even though this picture is of Fred Noll, Sr. and his wife Margaret in the early 1930s, it hadn't changed much when I went there in the '50s to buy baseball cards. Some Lanphier students got their lunches there since it was only a block south of the school, in the Rabbit Row neighborhood. [Courtesy of Helen Noll Deverman, their granddaughter]

This is the part of the "Avenue" that attracted most of us kids. "Couts," on the left, was the ice cream hang-out. Next to it was the Pantheon Theater where we began our movie watching—double features plus a cartoon for just a quarter. On the right was Watt Brothers' Pharmacy, where friendly Johnnie Watt held court. [The 1946 *Lan-Hi* staff dedicated its annual to the Avenue]

The North Branch of Lincoln Library was on the Avenue. When I was in school it was a great place to hang out as well as study. You had to whisper or they'd kick you out. That library was where I first got to love books and reading. I can still remember the book smell as you first walked in.

1958 [Courtesy of Sangamon County Tax Assessor Office]

Kohlrus' Grocery Store was located at 15th & Converse Ave., just a couple of blocks N.E. from LHS. It was typical of the many local corner grocery stores of that era that dotted local neighborhoods. c. 1940. [Courtesy of Johnnie Kohlrus]

The neighborhood just south of Reservoir Park called Rabbit Row was a tight-knit group of working class people. Rabbit Row Stags & Family Reunions were an annual affair from 1949 through most of the '70s. This one from the Fifties includes my dad, who was known to his boyhood friends as "Chink" (3rd row in front of the right post), and his brother Harley (2nd row in front of the left post). Burgoo and beer were the staples. [Courtesy of Helen Noll Deverman]

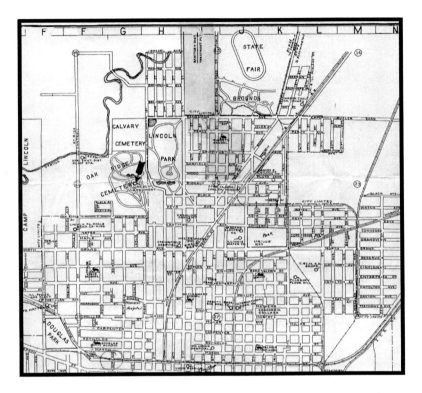

Springfield's "North End" is as much a state of mind as a place. Still, we have to define its boundaries somehow, so this 1948 map will take in most of it—from the Fair Grounds on the north to MacArthur (West Grand) Ave. on the west to Grandview on the east to Carpenter St. on the south. This artificial boundary is probably close to Lanphier's in that period. For you citizens who live beyond these points and who have the North End spirit, you are North Enders too. [Courtesy of Sangamon Valley Collection]

Bunn Grade School c. 1915, around the time my dad attended it. Most students from Bunn went on to Lanphier. Just two blocks south of LHS, its vacant property has been used as Lanphier's sports practice field since the school was torn down in the 1970s. Bunn, Palmer and Lawrence were all the same design—"sister schools." [Courtesy Sangamon Valley Collection]

Chapter 2

Background of Springfield's School System

The city of Springfield was created by enabling legislation in 1821—just three years after Illinois achieved statehood. Its first school, a log cabin, came into being three years later, with Andrew Orr as its first teacher. The next school, another log cabin structure, was built in 1828. I don't know what grades those early schools supported, but I would guess they were the one-room schools that were composed of children from first grade through what we nowadays call high school.

In 1854, the Springfield School Board was established to maintain free schools for the education of "all white" persons between the ages of five and twenty-one. This established the authority to organize the first public schools which would be under the control of a Board of School Inspectors and, of course, it reinforced the concept of separate schools for blacks.

The Board's first elementary school opened on April 14, 1856. The following year it decided to establish a high school, which was attended by 42 pupils. However, the Board rented various buildings for the high school until it built one in 1865, the year the Civil War ended. This first Springfield High School was constructed on Fourth and Madison at a cost of $65,000—a large amount of capital at the time—which demonstrated the importance of universal schooling for its citizenry.

A sad commentary on our city was that African-Americans' educational facilities were relegated to a shanty at the rear of a black church because of the "whites only" regulation. That law was struck down in 1873, thus opening public schools to all children.

A larger high school was built in 1897 to accommodate the growth of many commercial jobs in and around Springfield. Central High School, sometimes called Springfield High for continuity, had a capacity of 800 students and was built at a cost of $80,000. It was located at Adams and College. However, within 18 years, "Central" was so congested and in such poor condition that a bond issue was approved by voters in 1915 to construct a new high school to replace it.

In the fall of 1917, Springfield High School, the new flagship of education in the capital city, was opened on the west end of town, at 101 Lewis Street, where it remains today in its expanded form. It cost the taxpayers at the time a staggering half million dollars, and almost doubled the capacity of its predecessor building. Ironically, the city block on which SHS sits was the picturesque Forest Park where the first log cabin school in Sangamon County had been built almost a century before. Most Springfield High students know that their school was built on what was earlier Hutchinson's Cemetery and that some human bones still lie under the school's foundation, giving rise to ghoulish conjecture.

Here's the back story to the haunted school stories that spring up every Halloween, told by Linda Reed, former SHS librarian, in 2001 on Springfield High's website:

After the [log cabin] school had disappeared, the good church people erected there a little white church and buried their dead in the churchyard. Long after the church disappeared, graves and tombstones remained. The Park Board transformed it into Forest park. [It] was turned over to the School Board causing the bodies to be removed and [re]buried in Oak Ridge Cemetery. At the present time, the bones of some worthy are still at rest beneath the foundations of our school.

What became of Central High? Well, it turned into a de facto junior high for SHS for several years, where underclassmen and women usually took their class work. My mother, in fact, attended it for commercial classes in 1924 and then walked five minutes west to take her classical courses at Springfield High. Later, Central High School was converted into business offices. I went to the Board of Education offices there in 1955, shortly before it was razed, when Mom got my sister Sandy's temporary work permit (at 15). Mom waxed nostalgic as she gave us a tour through the venerable old high school building.

Springfield was growing rapidly enough to justify another high school the following decade. Built on the east side of town, Feitshans High School was constructed in 1929 on the same grounds where the Feitshans Elementary School had been serving east-side kids since 1886. It served the community for almost 40 years until it was replaced by Springfield Southeast High School in 1967. A third high school was contemplated on the north end even as Feitshans was handling the overcrowding on the east side. That of course was Lanphier.

My dad's favorite picture of his beloved Reservoir Park, with Watch Factory in the foreground. I gave a copy of it to the Sangamon Valley Collection and they inserted the various descriptives. c. Late 1920s. "Memorial Pool" (lower lf.) opened on Jun 17, 1928. [Courtesy of Sangamon Valley Collection and Julian P. Mitchell]

Chapter 3

Reservoir Park Controversy

Now for the rest of the story about Lanphier's inauspicious start. There was no objection to a third high school; everyone realized Springfield needed to serve the expanding North End. As a matter of fact, it was the citizens themselves who initiated the call for a high school for their children. The Northside Improvement Association was an active civic group that had a well-deserved reputation for promoting various North-End projects for many years. At the December 30, 1929 meeting of the NIA, it was officially recorded that "they would strive in the coming year to get a north-side high school" [*The Lanphier Light*, Vol. I, April 1, 1937]. In subsequent meetings it was decided that the new school would begin as a part of the Converse School, close to the proposed site in Reservoir Park on 11th Street and North Grand Avenue.

However, the public—especially the North Enders— felt their beloved park, which they affectionately called "Old Rizzy," should have been preserved, not torn down, for a school which could have been built on numerous other sites in the area. Even when I grew up there were many acres of undeveloped land within a mile or two of the proposed site.

One man who was around back then told me that school officials were afraid to build the school elsewhere on the north side because there were so many coal mine passages all over the place which could subside any time. Another argument for using the park for the school was that it would have been difficult and expensive to move all that dirt that comprised the reservoir to another location, in order to retain those lagoons. Finally, there was brought up the issue of safety as several people drowned in the reservoir over the years from inadequate fencing.

Notwithstanding my prejudices for keeping the park that was drummed into my young mind by my father, I can see that these arguments carried with them some reasonable weight. Still, like my father, I wish Reservoir Park could have been preserved and enhanced as a practical historic gem of those days gone by. Like the Orpheum Theatre and other pre-preservation monuments of our past, the park would never have been destroyed with the present-day civic consciousness.

The iconic Reservoir Park was built in 1866 around the need for a reservoir as part of the original water supply for Springfield's 20,000 residents and later as an emergency source of city water in case the pumping station at the Sangamon River failed.

The four-million-gallon reservoir itself was placed on the western most end of the park, with two lagoons, north and west of it, from which the dirt had been borrowed for the construction of the 33-foot high structure that defined and dominated the park. [See my book *Rabbit Row: The Life and Times of J.P. Mitchell*, 2004, Chapter 6, for a detailed history and description of Reservoir Park. Also see Howard Hohne's recollections of it—"A Boy's Park"— in the Appendix.] It is a sad fact that few living Springfieldians ever heard of this gem of a park or where it was located.

Over the years, the city park district enhanced the park into a postcard setting. (Literally, because post cards that depicted various bucolic scenes in the park were common around town during the 1920s.) My father was raised just south of Reservoir Park in a working class neighborhood called Rabbit Row—because its denizens had so many children. (One family had 21 children in one house!) During my growing-up years in the 1950s, Dad would bring up the subject of the park many times. He described it as the most beautiful park in Springfield, though not as large as "North Park" (Lincoln Park) or Washington Park.

It had a ballpark on the east end (which stands to this day within a modern stadium), and there were sidewalks, croquet fields, horseshoe pits, and several other fields to play ball and other games. On the north side there was a tennis court next to a play area with swings, a set of monkey bars and a seesaw. (My mom wanted to play on the swings on her way home from Converse School but her parents forbade her lest she run into bad elements, i.e., ornery non-Italian boys.)

On Sunday afternoons, Dad would see people rowing their rental boats leisurely on the shallow lagoons. In the winter they would skate on them. He went into rich detail about the many bushes, shrubs and other lush landscaping throughout the park. With a twinkle in his eye, he explained, "Hell, you couldn't walk next to any of them bushes without stepping on the legs of couples necking under them."

I was giving a talk about the park and the Rabbit Row neighborhood one evening to the Sangamon County Historical Society when not one, but two park neighbors brought to the meeting models they had painstakingly built to remind them of their young days in the park. That's how much that park meant to those people. Can you believe it, detailed *models*?

Those two enthusiasts plus the entire North End were up in arms when it was announced in 1926 that the park district was going to transfer the park to the school district. What precipitated the decision were plans on the drawing board to construct a 4,300-acre lake impoundment southeast of Springfield (Lake Springfield) as its new water supply, and therefore eliminating further need for the reservoir.

Johnnie Kohlrus, who along with his two brothers owned a grocery store on the east end of the park (across the tracks at 15th and Converse), told me this a few years back: "To give you an idea how emotional the issue was, when Norm Woods, a worker at Hummers, complained loudly [about plans to tear down the park], his job was threatened." What really got under Kohlrus' skin was that the park was originally donated to the city by Henry Converse "for recreational purposes only," (Kohlrus' words) thus making the building of a school on it inappropriate and probably illegal. Sangamon Valley Collection staff said that phrase was never in the conveyance.

He added that if they wanted a school in that area of the city, the school board could have built just a block north on a large field we used to call the Circus Grounds, now a four-ball diamond recreational area called David T. Lawless Park. (When Lanphier arranged to use it for overflow P.E. classes and a practice field in the early '70s, the coaches dubbed it the "Thorn Bowl," because it had been overgrown with weeds.) There was also a field the same size just west across the street that could have been part of a school complex.

Kohlrus wrote about the park in his wonderful 2007 memoir *Family*:

> Talking about old Reservoir Park— that was the center of entertainment. I think the North End took the biggest jipping [sic] when they got rid of that park. I don't care whether they said there were skeletons in the ground or not. [Apparently, some people drowned in the reservoir, one was a baby, and when they drained it, they found some skeletons.] They should have never of [sic] closed that park down. But, that's the way politics go, the boys got the land from up in the WPA (public works) deal and built the school, and that was the end of it. Those politicians cheated the North End out of a great park.

I recently asked Johnnie, now 88 and still candid and feisty, if there was a public outcry over destroying the park. He responded, "People didn't get together like that back then. No, there was no great public outcry. Hell, it wouldn't have made any difference anyway. They [politicians] got it for nothing anyway." Howard Hoehn, who grew up just across the street from the park, responded this way: "You've got to remember it was the Depression days back then. There was no work—it took me a year after high school to find a job. Nobody had the ability in that situation to holler about such things. We were trying to survive."

The powers-that-be wanted the school *there* and they got their way. In the fall of 1933, the school district directed the city's WPA workers, fresh from completing Lake Springfield, to finish razing the huge reservoir and fill the picturesque lagoons with the thousands of barrels of dirt that had been borrowed years before. "Over one hundred men used shovels, spades, wheelbarrows and picks to do this work over a several-week period," Howard Hoehn, 97, recalled as a personal witness to what he considered the destruction.

Dad never forgave the city fathers and its apathetic citizens. He was working in Chicago at the time and did not see the newspaper article about opening Lanphier High School. In part it read, "There was still quite a bit of water in the basement, residue of the reservoir seeping up from the ground." Dad probably would have wished the whole school had collapsed into a sinkhole. When I was a child and we passed by the school in our car, I heard Dad many, many times rail against tearing down his beautiful park with choice cuss words.

The "Jewel of the North End": Reservoir Park around 1900. This postcard shows the iconic fountain to the left of the picture with the pavilion in the center-right. For many years the park was the most popular place of recreation in the city. [Courtesy Sangamon Valley Collection]

The Reservoir Park ball stadium on the opening day of the 1927 season, on April 28. The new stadium's maiden day opening was two years earlier on May 13, 1925. It wasn't renamed Lanphier Ball Park until a decade later. [Courtesy Sangamon Valley Collection]

A popular winter activity at Reservoir Park was ice skating. This picture was taken around 1903 and shows the pavilion in the background. [Courtesy of the *Illinois State Journal-Register*]

The water fountain on top of the 33-foot rectangular reservoir. The ornate structure was the focal point of the entire Reservoir Park, especially when it spewed water through its fluted pipe when lights illuminated the spray. [Courtesy Sangamon Valley Collection]

This lovely picture is from the turn of the century. It shows children boating on the west Lagoon ("Duck Pond") that went dry in the '20s and was then called the "Dry Hollow." [Courtesy Sangamon Valley Collection]

The north steps of the reservoir in Reservoir Park. 1917
[*Il State Register* from Allan Dietz Cornelius (rt. front)]

Converse Grade School, at 7th Street and Eastman Ave., around the time it also housed the new North-End Converse High School (1930-1936) that became Lanphier High School

Chapter 4

The Beginning of LHS

Converse Grade School, located near Eighth Street and Eastman Avenue, just three blocks west of Reservoir Park, had been a North-End fixture since 1892. My mother, Zania ("Jennie) Rose Antonacci-Roscetti, and her siblings attended it after a house fire forced her family to move from Starnes (a small village of 22 families and a school on the north edge of Grandview that nobody remembers today) to 1809 East Converse.

As mentioned before, what was to be called Lanphier High School had its beginning at the Converse School building in the school year 1930-1931, when the school board added ninth grade to Converse to alleviate the flood of North-End students into Springfield High and Feitshans High. Mr. Samuel H. Heidler was principal at the time. Planning on yet another high school, the school board added tenth grade to Converse in 1934, then eleventh and twelfth grades the following two years, respectively.

George Stickney was reassigned from Lawrence Elementary to Converse High School (i.e. that part of Converse set apart from the grade school classes) as its principal in 1934 to oversee the transition from the Converse school building to what would come to be called Lanphier. Here is how the *Lan-Hi* (the school annual or yearbook) staff described the hand-off in its 1938 edition: "During the year

[1935] it was decided that a new high school was needed to take care of the large enrollment. Enthusiasm ran high as the students realized that they were going to have a new high school the following year."

Converse Grade School itself was beginning to be phased out during this same period with its pupils going to the other five area elementary schools. When it closed its doors for good in 1939, the school district was working on plans to rent it out to Cathedral Boys High School which had begun operations in 1930, with 90-some students, sharing space in the downtown St. Mary's Elizabeth school. Cathedral leased Converse School in 1940 and later purchased it (and added a stand-alone gymnasium on the south side). It moved to its present location on the far west side of Springfield in 1959 as Griffin High School, named after the Bishop who had opened Cathedral 21 years earlier.

Naming the School

The school board named the new high school after Robert C. Lanphier, Sr., president and cofounder of Sangamo Electric Company (See next chapter), a large electrical instrument factory just west of Lanphier High School, across Eleventh Street, to show its appreciation for his considerable help in obtaining needed funds by organizing and spearheading a bond issue. Had it not been for Lanphier's efforts in getting the bond issue passed, it is likely there would not have been a Lanphier High School, at least not before WWII.

There were several standout athletes who came out of the Converse High School tradition, but two extraordinary ones who must be mentioned or its history would not be complete are "Rocket" Ray Ramsey and Jim LaRocca. Ray Ramsey—also called "Rabbit Ray" because of his agility—is regarded by local sports editor Jim Ruppert as "the most versatile athlete Springfield has ever produced." [See "A Tribute to Ray Ramsey" in the Appendix.] Another player of note is Jim LaRocca ('37), who played football and basketball for three years at Converse and Lanphier and was All-City in football.

Robert was the son of John C. Lanphier, an attorney in Springfield and the grandson of Charles H. Lanphier, the Civil War editor and eventual owner of the *Illinois State Register*. (Charles H. Lanphier is credited by one newspaper writer with helping to draft legislation that started the Springfield Public Schools.) In addition to mustering support for financing the school, Mr. Lanphier, an 1894 graduate of Springfield High School, donated the public address system to the new school, no small item in that era. At the astronomical cost of $2,000 (the annual salary for the average North Ender was about half of that), it was a combination of a two-way speaker to every classroom plus a radio hookup for broadcasts a state-of-the-art communication system back then. An alumnus from that time told me that the students loved that PA system: "We were the only school that had a public address system. It was a really big deal. We sat in our classrooms and got to hear all the announcements from the staff. Students even used it for the various clubs. You could hear it in the halls and outside. It was really something in those days."

The school district's website tells us in the Lanphier History section that "The name Lanphier was the last name of the family who owned the land on which our school sits." It also points out that "the French word Lanphier means 'Land on Fire.'"

That first statement about the family owning the Reservoir Park property early on is inaccurate based on the Sangamon Valley Collection records. The abstracts in the Deed Books show a chain of title that does not include any Lanphier family ownership. The entire tract that was to become Reservoir Park (and eventually a portion of the site of Lanphier High School) was owned by John Irwin in the early years of the city. He sold it as two separate parcels a few years later (July 6, 1848) to Henry Converse [Book CC, p. 214], who in turn sold the 30 acres to the Springfield Waterworks on September 28, 1866 for the reservoir [Book 29, p.164]. The city-owned Waterworks eventually conveyed it to the park district and from there to the school board which still owns it.

Prior to naming the high school after Mr. Lanphier, the park board floated the idea of renaming Reservoir Park after him. He shied away from the idea and suggested instead that it be renamed Sangamo Park. [*Springfield Journal*, June 15, 1934, p. 11] However, it must have happened because a year later the same paper had an article [Dec. 10, 1935, p.1] stating that "Lanphier Park" will be deeded over to the school board sometime that week. It went on to announce that $727,000 would be allocated to several building projects, including Lanphier High School ($300,000) and a Feitshans High School addition ($170,000).

Why they even bothered to rename the park remains a mystery considering it had already been decided to tear it down. My dad would cynically have concluded that it was a political step to lessen the blow of razing his park. It is more likely that it was simply to retain the name for the baseball stadium (opened in 1925 where the 3-I League played), called "Lanphier Park, now under the auspices of the Park District." In 1977, it was renamed "Robin Roberts Stadium in Lanphier Park," as a tribute to the Lanphier graduate and Springfield's most accomplished baseball player.

The distinctive tower and the massive clock stand sentry over the main entrance of the Illinois Watch Company. c. 1930s [Courtesy of the Sangamon Valley Collection]

Chapter 5

Two Major North-End Employers

The following is an important story that may clear up confusion between the names of two closely related neighbors of our high school and two important North-End industries: the Illinois Watch Company and the Sangamo Electric Company, which were sometimes erroneously used interchangeably when talking about their location across the street from Lanphier.

The Illinois Watch Company

The Illinois Watch Company was founded in 1870 by a group of owners, among them   J.C. Adams, the promoter, John W. Bunn, the backer, and attorney John Todd Stuart, its first president. After the Panic of 1873, it was reorganized and then reorganized again in 1878 when Bunn put his older brother, Jacob Bunn, Sr., into the company as president, and produced the first open-faced watch in the United States. One year later, it manufactured the first nickel watch movement. "In 1903, the company began manufacturing specialty high-grade railroad movements that have become collectors' items today—the Sangamo Special, the Bunn Special and the A. Lincoln." [*The Springfield Journal-Register*'s insert, May 8, 1984]

The "Watch Factory," as I always knew it, grew under the older brother's leadership into one of the premier railroad watch manufacturers in the country and around the world. Standard railroad time was synonymous with the Illinois Watch Company pocket watch. At its height the watch factory employed 1,500 people in its Springfield factory; many of them were women and most of them North Enders. It even had its own band and girls softball team, the Bloomer Girls.

In the southwest corner of the block (near the present day McDonald's) was erected a stone observatory during the 1912-1913 period, which became a Springfield landmark for many years. Its purpose, according to Robert "Bob" Lanphier III, was "for determining the time accurately [in setting watches]...In those years there were no atomic clocks or National Time signals transmitted from Denver." The ornate stone observatory itself was unfortunately torn down, but its updated telescope was saved and erected in a garage-like structure on the Boy Scouts "Camp Bunn," southwest of Springfield. One of the two original telescopes ended up at Bradley University and eventually in a Peoria park where it is in use today.

Jacob Bunn, Jr. took over the reins of leadership in 1897 and continued the company's growth. After Bunn, Jr.'s death in 1926, the company's leadership decided to get out of the watch business and concentrate on the developing Sangamo effort, discussed below. It sold the company to Hamilton Watches in 1927. The corporate sale was partially crafted by Watch Company vice president, Willard Bunn, Sr., a grandson of Jacob Bunn, Sr. Hamilton paid $5 million ($67 million today) for the Illinois Watch Company, a valuable investment for the financially savvy Bunns. It should be noted that the family sold the Watch Company for cash, not stock, which was good timing and the right medium of exchange since, during the tough Depression which followed, about the last thing a person needed was a new watch or watch company stock. And it was this cash that allowed the family to invest more capital into the Springfield Marine Bank and other interests in the early '30s.

By 1932, the Great Depression forced Hamilton to close the Illinois factory, though they retained possession of the brand name. What has stood the test of time is the large clock on the original Watch Factory's tower facing 9th Street: it is still there today, although not always as dependable as the watches that were produced by the renowned Illinois Watch Company. Farrell Gay, a local businessman and avid collector of Illinois watches, pointed out that "the original clock/movement from the tower was no longer in place…We found a movement (which I still have) that had a date written on it of 1956. I do not recall but, but [the investment group] probably promptly replaced that movement with another current model for [IEPA]."

Sangamo Electric Company

In the mid -1890s, Jacob Bunn, Jr. became acquainted with a German inventor in Peoria, Illinois, named Ludwig Gutman, and was intrigued by his concept for a meter to measure electrical power. Such a meter would require the skilled labor and precision gears and parts such as were in precision watches. But Jacob Bunn, Sr. was so cool on the idea that he let his son do the investing. The elder Bunn was likely gun shy, remembering the financial collapse that he and his investors endured in the Panic of 1873, in which he, reputed to be one of the richest men in Illinois after the Civil War, had lost most of his wealth. [Read about "The Bunn Miracle" in the Appendix. Also read there "The Enterprising Bunn Brothers," about their many business interests.]

In 1897, Bunn, Jr. met Robert C. Lanphier, a recent graduate from Yale University in electrical engineering (with high honors) who had a job offer back East with the General Electric Company. At a fortuitous dinner party on July 4th, Bunn asked the young Yalie to look at Gutman's concept and see if there was any possibility of a successful business. Lanphier also became intrigued with the idea of measuring electrical power and agreed to work on the project during that summer at the Watch Company.

After getting into the project, Lanphier was so enthralled that he threw caution to the wind and turned down the job with General Electric. (In the fall of 1897, Jacob Bunn, Sr. suddenly passed away at work, and so Bunn, Jr. assumed the presidency of the Illinois Watch Company.) Over the next fifteen months, Bunn, Gutman and Lanphier developed a working model of the meter and put together a business plan to manufacture and sell one of the first induction watt-hour meters to measure electrical power.

In January 1899, they organized the Sangamo Electric Company with Jacob Bunn, Jr. as secretary-treasurer, his brother Henry Bunn as president, Gutman as first vice-president, Lanphier as general manager, and Otis White as general superintendent. Lanphier was given carte-blanche by Bunn to ramrod the fledging business to its full potential. In 1926 Lanphier succeeded Jacob Bunn Jr. as president of Sangamo.

Originally conducting business as an arms-length division of the Illinois Watch Company, the "Meter Department," as Sangamo was called the first three years, eventually succeeded despite many trials and errors, under the Bunn-Lanphier-White partnership and fast became an international manufacturer of electric meters and other electric products. (Lanphier named the company after the Illini Indian chief.) When the watch factory was sold just before the national economy tanked, Sangamo took over its entire factory complex and played an important role in producing military electrical products during WWII and after. Most Springfieldians would be surprised to know that Sangamo Electric designed 90 percent of all our shipboard anti-submarine SONAR equipment and manufactured 50 percent of it at its Springfield factory during the war.

So, these two major North-End employers coexisted as related entities on the same city block complex, sometimes sharing the same buildings, for 33 years—from 1899 through 1932. (Actually, the watch factory's buildings were clustered more toward the west side of the block facing 9th Street, while Sangamo eventually grew from the east side of the block facing 11th Street. Of course, Sangamo inherited the entire four-city blocks after 1932.)

When I was growing up in the post-war years, some of my relatives and most of my neighbors worked at the "Meter Works," which was one of the city's biggest employers. Two neighbors, Mr. Delaney and Mr. Hull, were two Sangamo managers who wore suits and ties to work. I was impressed to see them walking the half-mile to their jobs every day. (I was even more impressed to see, on my way to school, Mrs. Delaney kiss her husband good-bye each morning as she handed him his lunch at the door, just a few houses down from our house on East Converse Avenue.) The other thing I remember about Sangamo from my youngest years forward was its familiar factory whistle, a piercing stream-powered sound you could hear for miles that announced changes in shifts during the day and night. It was a reassuring sound to North Enders that all was well with our local economy.

Always mindful of the welfare of its workers, Sangamo began issuing "service warrants" to its workers in 1935, so they could receive cash in the same amount as stockholders. The next year it began paying workers Christmas bonuses and continued it as business conditions allowed. Early to acknowledge the principal of collective bargaining, Sangamo recognized the SELCO Employees Association in 1937 as the bargaining agency for wages and worker conditions. The next year the company replaced the warrant plan in favor of a pension plan with Travelers Insurance, with a 50-50 contribution and automatic retirement at age 65. It was not until the end of 1944 that other unions also were formed within the company. Management and employees had a harmonious relationship until the 1960s when it became more contentious. Steve Rambach, a Lanphier teacher, told me he would have his students stand at the windows and watch striking workers congregate in front of Sangamo in the 1970s. "Our history classes had a front row seat to discuss labor relations and terms such as 'scabs,' 'picket lines,' and 'collective bargaining.' The labor strife lasted for four or five years."

Still, Sangamo was a great place to work and helped many North Enders earn respectable livings. Bob Lanphier

recalled the annual fall Sangamo Company-sponsored picnic
at the Fairgrounds:

> It was a great time. It was really an
> employees appreciation day. Ask some old
> timers about it for the book. [I couldn't find
> any.] It started around noon on a Saturday
> and went late into the night with dancing and
> singing. There were food and games, pie
> eating and tasting contests. The Brass Hats,
> the executive team, played softball against
> the employees…everybody watched it. There
> was a big beer tent too. This annual event
> began before WWII and went into the early
> '60s. The employees and their families loved
> it.

When Mr. Lanphier died at his home in 1939 at age
61, his assistant, Donald Funk, took over the presidency of
Sangamo, and in 1952 his son Charles ("Chick") H.
Lanphier succeeded Mr. Funk. (Mr. Lanphier's other son
and namesake was heading up the British company in
London when his father died.) Robert Davies succeeded
Chick in the early seventies. Sangamo remained a stable and
successful enterprise under these capable leaders, but, like
so many other companies of that era, it fell prey to the
mergers and acquisitions craze, and in 1975 it was acquired
by the French conglomerate, Schlumberger Electric
Company. Three years later Schlumberger merged Sangamo
with Weston Instruments of New Jersey, forming Sangamo
Weston.

In the summer of 1978, the Springfield factory was
closed and Sangamo Weston was moved to Georgia and

Florida, thereby sealing the fate of the 75-year-old North-End employer. The Georgia plant was shut down for good in 1985, and Sangamo was no more. The Springfield plant was purchased by an investment group the following year and, as one of the investors told me, they "leased space in various parts of the plant to a number of different entities, including Caterpillar of Peoria...Pease's Candy and the Illinois Environmental Agency...In [around] 1996 we turned it over to the IEPA." The agency consolidated most of its Springfield officers there, and today it hardly resembles the robust factory I would pass on my bike as a youngster. As my 102-year-old mother regretted a few years back when she waxed philosophical about changes in Springfield, "Kenneth, nothing stays the same around here."

From reading Robert C. Lanphier's memoir about his company, *40 Years of Sangamo: 1896-1936* and other research information, I garnered some insight into his personality and character. His writing revealed an honest and humble businessman who felt lucky to have been the driving force behind Sangamo becoming an international leader in the electric instrumentation business.

Giving credit to his mentor and business partner, he emphasized over and over again how kind and helpful Mr. Bunn was in guiding him along the path of success. The dedication page in his book says it all: "Affectionately Dedicated to the man whose faith, courage and judgment made Sangamo possible—Jacob Bunn."

Many people who heard the name Lanphier in connection with Sangamo probably did not realize that "he was recognized for many years as one of the foremost electrical engineers in the United States and his counsel

often was sought by research experts in that field."
[*Springfield Journal*, January 29, 1939, p. 1]

That same quoted article in the morning paper went on to observe that "during Lanphier's long career in electrical engineering, he was associated with a number of world famous men, including Thomas Edison and Charles F. Kettering, vice president of General Motors, in charge of the research division of that vast company." [See the next chapter for more on the Lanphier-Kettering relationship.] And, of course, the list of famous inventors and engineers includes Walter D'Arcy Ryan, the illuminating engineer.

Here is how local historian Benjamin Pratt Thomas summarized Lanphier's professional life in *Sangamo: A History of 50 Years* [page 112]:

> Lanphier's death... came on January 29, 1939. His passing marked the end of an era for Sangamo, for he was the last of that illustrious trio of Bunn, Lanphier and White, who had so ably guided the company during its difficult years. The brain and heart of the company since he succeeded Jacob Bunn as president upon the latter's death in 1926, Mr. Lanphier had followed in the traditions of Mr. Bunn's organizational and managerial genius to demonstrate in abundant measure the qualities essential to successful business management. Patient and considerate toward his fellow officers and employees, he had inspired devotion and respect. A pioneer in the field of meter development, his brilliance as an inventor and technician was recognized throughout the engineering world. The city of Springfield mourned his loss no less than

Sangamo, for he was active in many movements for civic betterment.

Of course one of Lanphier's crowning achievements in Springfield's "civic betterment" was his promoting the building of the North-End's own school which fittingly bears his name.

The Illinois Watch Company—Sangamo Electric Company complex over-looking Reservoir Park. The Observatory was located in a prominent location for all to see. Bob Lanphier III surmised that part of the reason was to "impress customers with the IWC's technical competencies." c. 1925 [Courtesy of the Sangamon Valley Collection of the Springfield Lincoln Library]

A supervisor talking to some of his employees at the Watch Factory.
c. 1924 [Courtesy of the Sangamon Valley Collection]

The long-gone iconic Illinois Watch Factory Observatory. Built around 1913, it was likely made from stone provided by the Springfield Culver Stone Company, which went out of business the same year. It was probably larger and more ornate than it needed to be, but it was a beautiful North-End landmark. [Courtesy of the Sangamon Valley Collection]

The original telescope from the Illinois Watch Factory still in use at the Northmoor Observatory on a golf course in Peoria, IL. It was transferred to Bradley University in the early '30. The local astronomical society found it under the practice gym bleachers and restored it. The 8-1/4" scope was built by O.L. Petitdidier of Chicago. The Equatorial mounting was designed and built by the IWC itself. [Courtesy of the Northmoor Observatory and the Peoria Astronomical Society]

Jacob W. Bunn, Jr., who made the Illinois Watch Co. and Sangamo Electric Co. into huge successes. [Courtesy of the Sangamon Valley Collection]

Sangamo Electric Company, as one of Springfield's largest employers, in the 1950s. Notice its neighbor at the top, Lanphier High School, before its expansion and before the Thomas Edison Junior High School was built. [Courtesy of Sangamon Valley Collection]

The Bunns were the dominant players in the formation and management of what came to be the Illinois Watch Company. John was one of the original backers of the company and was its vice-president. His older brother, Jacob (left) eventually became president. When he passed away, his son, Jacob Bunn, Jr. (right) took over the reigns. c.1885. [Courtesy of the Sangamon Valley Collection]

Robert C. Lanphier at his dapper best
[*Illinois State Journal*, Jan. 29, 1939, p. 1]

Chapter 6

A Personal Glimpse into Robert C. Lanphier

One of my goals in writing this book is to give you a more intimate picture of Robert Lanphier, the person. Before I began this book, the only two things I knew about Mr. Lanphier were that he had been the president of Sangamo and our high school's namesake, having seen the austere formal portrait of him hanging over the entrance hall. I asked his two surviving grandchildren to give me some idea of what their grandfather was like from stories their parents told about him. Here is what Nancy Lanphier Chapin emailed me:

> As I told you, I never met him, as I was born in '38 and my parents left me in England when they came back that last year. I'm told he was a wonderful, warm man who was loved by all (Isn't that the story of everyone's grandfather?). He had cancer of the larynx for years and his voice box was replaced with a mechanical one. He just kept on working and supporting the community throughout.
>
> My mother-in-law said that she served on the Child and Family Service Board during this period and would be his intermediary as his 'whispers' could not be heard very far, but he kept on contributing. My family [members] were also amazed years later when the families of employees of Sangamo would return a portrait of him that

had been preserved since his death until that person died. Evidently the pictures were prized.

He had an engineer's inquiring mind. There was an article in [the] *IT* many years ago about a light show he engineered here after seeing one in California. I'll attach the story.

The article she was referring to was in the *Illinois Times* ["Robert Lanphier lights up Springfield" on June 10, 2004]. Writer Bob Cavanagh described how Mr. Lanphier brought back a light show idea he saw at the San Francisco Exposition in 1915 created by Walter D'Arcy Ryan, famed illuminating engineer. He was so excited by it that he talked the Springfield Commercial Association and others into displaying a huge railroad engine on the south lawn of the Old Courthouse. Its steam plume was washed with colored spotlights and enhanced with mirrors to produce "a magnificent, shimmering, multihued nighttime rainbow," which the public loved. Such was Lanphier's lifelong interest in anything inventive and inspiring.

Among Mr. Lanphier's many community activities—and one of the reasons the board of education saw fit to name the new high school after him— were the following: an organizer of the Associated Welfare agencies; a long-time member of the Rotary Club; a director of the local Red Cross; vice president of the Family Welfare Association; a member of the Board of Elders of the First Presbyterian Church; a trustee of Illinois College in Jacksonville; and a director of the Marine Bank. These are just a few of what he would have considered civic duties he participated in to make Springfield a better place to live.

The most important tribute to him as a person came from the employees at Sangamo themselves. The front page banner story of Mr. Lanphier's passing (at home) made mention of how his employees felt about him: It said that "they rewarded him with a loyalty that was akin to devotion." That's as nice a farewell as they come.

Here's how someone remembered the day of his burial at Oak Ridge Cemetery, in a retrospective on Mr. Lanphier's life: "Well-wishers were so numerous at Lanphier's funeral in 1939, the overflow crowd was invited to the [Lanphier] high school, where the ceremonies were aired over the public address system that had been paid for by Lanphier." [*State Journal-Register*, by Natalie Boehme, April 29, 1994.]

He had four brothers, John C., Jr., from Springfield; Commander Alfred Young from New York City, a retired naval officer; Charles Goin, also living in Springfield; and James, who died as an infant. He had been married to his wife of 38 years when he passed away. She was Bertha Oliver Lanphier, from another prominent local family.

They had three sons and one daughter—Robert C., Jr., associated with the British Sangamo plant in England; Charles (Chick) H., also working in Sangamo's management; their oldest son, Edward, a brilliant student, who died while a senior at Yale [See in the Appendix the story about a scholarship for the Springfield public high schools in his honor.]; and Margaret DeWitt Smith, living in Canada with her husband, whom she had recently married.

Mr. Lanphier and his wife had five grandchildren. His mother, 84, was still living at the time of his death.

The newspaper pointed out only one of his several avocations: that "he was an inveterate traveler, making almost annual trips to England in the interests of British Sangamo, and making a number of world tours [with his wife.]" Nancy added that he loved gardening. He built a summer cottage in 1927 on a lake in Michigan. His family enjoyed the weeks at that retreat for many years.

Among Mr. Lanphier's papers in his summer home are documents and film about his two adventures he took with his personal friend, Charles Kettering. In the last chapter I wrote about his close business association with Kettering, who was a well-respected businessman of that era. He was also the holder of 186 patents, a research engineer, founder of Delco Company, and philanthropist (e.g., Sloan-Kettering Cancer Center in New York City). In 1930 Kettering invited Mr. Lanphier, along with several other friends, on a voyage on his yacht, the *Olive K*, to the Galapagos Islands by way of the Panama Canal. He took them on a second adventurous journey in 1932 to explore Chichen Itza and other Mayan ruins in the Yucatan.

Grandson and namesake of Mr. Lanphier, Robert C Lanphier III, gave me additional insights into his grandfather's personal life:

> RCL Sr's hobby was pottery, he loved the process and I have to feel that he found it very relaxing. He had a pottery wheel both in the basement of his home at 1632 Leland Ave in Springfield, and another up here at his home (where I now live) called 'Grey Gables'

on Glen Lake at Glen Arbor, Michigan. The 'wheel' here was located in the Boathouse where life could be quite tranquil. We have several pieces of his work here at Grey Gables. As my sister said, he loved his home, a beautiful place on a beautiful Lake, here in Michigan...as do I.

He was also quite fond of playing tennis and golf. He had a tennis court at his summer home so he played quite a bit when he vacationed here.

I have each of his diaries from 1894 through 1938, but they are mostly concerned with his activities with Sangamo and events, such as his children being born.

Bob loaned me a lovely, short autobiography of his great aunt's—Mr. Lanphier's daughter, Margaret [now] Wengren— who is 98 and living in Massachusetts at the time of this writing. Here are some excerpts from *Margaret Lanphier Wengren Remembers*, which will give you a flavor of the culture she grew up in and her dad's character:

It was a very privileged growing up in the sense of a modest neighborhood, right on the edge of town....You could walk an eighth of a mile down the street and you were in the Illinois countryside, in that land of the soybeans and corn.

...And my father was really a very brilliant engineer and devised several great improvements on this original German [electric meter] patent.

...I had a D in Physics [at Vassar]. And I had never gathered a D in my life before. And I had a cable from my father [who was in England] saying, "Margaret, you will cancel all social engagements until Physics mark improves."

...But my father, we knew, had terminal cancer. He had had his larynx removed...

...It was Depression time and [my father] said [if I tried to get a job after college] I would take work away from a woman who needed it and he could support me. I think his health had a lot to do with my not pushing that.

One of Mr. Lanphier's siblings, Alfred, graduated from the United States Naval Academy at Annapolis in 1910 and had a distinguished career as a naval officer. He wrote a hard-to-put-down memoir [*Autobiography*, Alfred Young Lanphier, CDR. USN/Ret/, 1970] mainly about his exploits and travels. However, in the part about his family he praises his brother, eight years his senior, as a paragon for his life. It's one of the kindest, most heartfelt tributes I have ever read from one brother to another:

The other big factor [that had a lasting effect on me] was my early, deep and permanent adoration of my oldest brother, Rob. Early in life I knew that I didn't have his mental equipment but as he had neither time nor any inclination for athletics I worked hard to make the teams. With lots of help from [my other brother] John Lanphier, I did pretty well and Rob would give me a smack from time to time and tell me I was going good. It sure sounded good to me. I think the reason I stuck it out at the Naval Academy was because I couldn't bear to think that Rob should believe that I did not have the brains or the guts or both to make it.

I had many, many other things to thank him for as long as he lived and as long as I will live. All over the world he would go a long way out of his way to come visit with me in whatever peculiar place I happened to be on duty and he always made a gala occasion when he came. He was the tops of all the few, almost flawless men, I have known.

When the school board named the new high school after Mr. Lanphier, it also adopted the following resolution that is a fitting conclusion to his life and an appropriate close to this section on the man:

We ask the school be named thus because Robert C. Lanphier, a lifelong citizen of Springfield, has over a long period of time continuously contributed to the welfare of the citizens and residents of the city of Springfield, organizing and assisting in the creation and maintenance of various agencies for the general welfare, giving generously thereto personal labor and financial assistance, and moreover, has supported and assisted the schools of Springfield and the opportunities of its people to obtain education and learning and the benefits thereof for themselves and their children.

"A steam locomotive, moved to the courthouse grounds, sent steam vapor to special plumes on the building. Colored floodlights lighted the escaping steam with an 'indescribably beautiful' effect," was the caption from the *Springfield: A Reflection in Photography* book, 2002. This of course was the doings of Robert C. Lanphier who brought back the idea from the San Francisco Exposition in 1915. [Courtesy of the Sangamon Valley Collection]

A Lanphier Family portrait, Lt. to Rt.: Robert and Bertha with their children: Robert, Jr., Edward, Charles ("Chick"), and Margaret. The Lanphiers were French Huguenots who fled repression by way of southern Ireland. Two centuries later they landed in Virginia, in 1732. c. 1921 [*Margret Lanphier Wengren Remembers*, March 1998]

The "Grey Gables," the summer home on Glen Lake near Glen Arbor, Michigan that Robert C. Lanphier built in 1928. This home was located in a secluded area where it became a retreat for him and for his family. His grandson, Robert C. Lanphier III, is now retired there year around. [Courtesy Robert C. Lanphier III]

Robert C. Lanphier with his namesakes: son and grandson.
Each a Yale graduate and each an electrical engineer.
[Courtesy of Robert C. Lanphier III]

Edward Oliver Lanphier. After his untimely death at 20, his parents created a scholarship to honor him that continues to this day. It is given at all three Springfield public high schools. See Appendix for the details about this prestigious Math and Science Prize. [Courtesy of Robert C. Lanphier III]

Robert C. Lanphier learned the art of pottery in the 1930s. These are examples of his work still at the Grey Gables in Michigan. He had two wheels, one in Springfield and one in his boat house at his summer home in Michigan. [Courtesy of Robert C. Lanphier III]]

The Avenue began at this point—9th and North Grand Avenue. William Crook, Jr., the local artist, drew this in 1958 as part of a special insert for the *Illinois State Journal Register*'s tribute to the North-End called "Springfield North Revisited...a Celebration." In addition to this print, Crook drew several others to illustrate North End subjects written about in the publication, promoted by the Springfield Marine Bank.

Chapter 7

Other North-End Businesses

Pillsbury Mills

Another close neighbor of Lanphier High School was "Pillsbury Mill"—we hardly ever pronounced it properly as plural—located just a few blocks to the southeast, on North 15ᵗʰ Street.

It was built adjacent to the C&IM railroad yard for required access to rail service since the wheat had to be shipped in and the finished product had to be shipped out. C&IM Rail Road itself was and is a North-End employer, with its rail yard and maintenance shops right there. My Grandfather Mitchell was a fireman with them for many back-breaking years. One of his sons was run over by their engines at 15th and North Grand. [For a description of the railroads and trains at that time, see my book *Rabbit Row*, Chapter 4, which recounts my grandfather's career as an engine fireman.]

The Mill immediately hired 300 employees when it began operations in 1930, at the beginning of the Depression. In its heyday after WWII, it employed 1,500 workers, most of them North Enders. When the Watch Factory closed its doors, many of its workers eagerly sought work at Pillsbury three years later.

Founded in Minneapolis, Minnesota in 1872, the family-owned Pillsbury and Company was the first flour mill in the country to use steel rollers for processing grain. It processed raw materials for use in a variety of kitchen foods, such as premixed ingredients for making cakes, pancakes, biscuits, muffins, pie crusts, gingerbread and other baked goods.

It grew to the point where the Springfield plant expanded its operation several times. In 1934, it added a 2 million bushel wheat storage elevator. The following year it added a fifth floor to the specialty building. In 1937 it built a nine-story building with a warehouse, feeders, sifters and a grinding department—all for a cool million dollars. In 1947 Pillsbury added its signature 300- by 180-foot, two-story building that was designed to take advantage of the company's three existing flour mills and specialty plant. When it opened in July 1949, the new facility was one of the most modern of its kind in the world and a boon to the North End. Flour was transferred pneumatically to storage bins, where it was held until needed. The physical plant was an impressive sight. Situated on 18 acres, it consisted of four or five warehouses, two flour mills with those tall storage elevators, a bakery mixing operation, and a five-story grain grocery plant.

Pillsbury was a North-End mainstay for seventy years. In 1991, it sold the plant to Cargill, which closed the facility down for good in 2001. It sold it to Ley Metal Recycling in 2008, with plans to salvage what they can. Once torn down, it will be replaced by who knows what, another casualty of modernity.

A recent article about the Mill in the *State Journal-Register* by Rich Saal refers to an earlier story on the plant in which a former Pillsbury worker, John Keller, described the aroma that it produced around the North End: "The neighborhood always smelled like a fresh-backed loaf of bread or donuts." That's exactly how I remember Pillsbury. That wonderful smell and the white cotton caps its employees wore along with their white uniforms.

International Shoe Company

Another major Springfield employer, just a few blocks south of Lanphier at 11th and Enos Streets, was the "shoe factory," a North-End fixture since the early 20th Century. Its plant complex was built as the Springfield Furniture Company (which made school and church furniture, starting in 1890), but was taken over by the Desnoyer Brothers Shoe Company in 1903. When it went bankrupt in 1910, it was taken over by the newly formed International Shoe Company.

One of its signature features was that most of its product was made by women. That caused controversy when an Illinois Senate Vice Commission called the working conditions at the shoe factory a "disgrace" in 1913. As the Sangamon County Historical Society website explained, "One 21-year-old woman told the commission that girls in the box department 'were driven at top speed, and that the foreman cursed them when they failed to turn out as much work as he desired.' *The New York Times* reported. 'On a half dozen different occasions, she testified, she fainted from excessive exertion. She said the foreman of the department sometimes seized girls and shook them when they displeased him.'"

The scandal resulted in better working conditions (such as women's restrooms) and representation by the Boot and Shoe Workers Union the next year. When I was growing up, it had a decent reputation as an acceptable place to work, albeit with low wages.

During the early 1930s, the shoe factory employed around 650 people to manufacture 4,500 pairs of shoes a *day*, a very real boon to the mainly North-End families that depended on the sparse wages for Depression Era day-to-day survival. Because of its location, it can be assumed that many of Lanphier students' mothers took work there throughout the years, and later students themselves.

Like most of the other major local industries, International Shoe had to reduce its workforce starting in the late 1950s. Employment fell to 300 by the 1960s, and the factory closed its doors for good in 1964, two years after I graduated from Lanphier. The facility found an important home when Goodwill Industries bought it. However, its future at that site is in question if the railroad relocation plans are carried out.

The Paint Factory

From what I could piece together, the paint factory started out as the Sullivan Springfield Paint Company (c.1930s) and then reorganized as the Springfield Paint Manufacturing Company (1951). Then it was sold and was called the Seck-DeVault Paint Manufacturing Company (1953) and finally the Kyanize Paints, Inc. (1960s). Its official address was North 14th Street and Ridgely Avenue.

Tony Ramirez, who grew up a couple blocks from it in the 1930s and 1940s, told me the Paint Factory ran adjacent to his street (North 14th) in Mill Row, which he called "an ethnic mix of families." He also said there was a large canning factory taking up a full city block to the west of the paint factory that was converted into a livestock auction house when he was a boy. I don't know how many employees worked for those two industries, but I would guess a hundred or so, adding to the North End's economic base.

My friends and I were intimately connected to the Paint Factory because it lay just north of our hang-out in the Cotton Woods, a small enclave of trees and brush sometimes occupied by hobos. We played war there and built our own forts. In July we lit our firecrackers away from parents' prying eyes. We would walk the old foundations of part of the plant that had been torn down. Its poured concrete walls were about 9 inches thick and 10 feet above the basement floors. We would see how fast we could negotiate the maze with our arms outstretched for balance. I don't know of anyone who fell.

The Avenue

At least as far back as my dad's era— in the teens and twenties, there was a long stretch of small businesses along both sides of brick-paved North Grand Avenue (hence the name "Avenue") from 9th Street to the tracks at 6th Street and even beyond. It was the North-End's shopping district before there were shopping centers and strip malls. Among the two dozen or more mom and pop businesses were Watt

Bros. Pharmacy, Noonan's Hardware, the Kerasotes' Pantheon Theatre, Hudson's Variety and Coutrakon's Confectionery. "Couts" (pronounced "coots") was the big after-school draw for Lanphier students. It had a soda fountain with cherry cokes, chocolate sodas, etc. and pool and snooker tables in the back room. Many customers felt its ten cent caramel apples were the best in town. And wedged in between stores in the second block was our North Branch Lincoln Library. I suppose this business district employed 100 or 125 North Enders, which added to the economy and to the ease of shopping, since many of these citizens shopped on foot. *The Springfield Journal-Register*'s May 5, 1984 supplement in a tribute to the North End describes the Avenue in wonderfully nostalgic narrative; here is a sample to sum up our sketch of it:

> But grocery shopping was not the only thing to do on the "Avenue." Fifty years ago, you could find as many as 30 businesses along the strip. Other than Dockhum & Dawson's [Grocery Store], there were Good's Grocery Store, Clark's Market and Layendecker's Meat Market. Amrhein's Bakery regularly filled the air with the wholesome aroma of freshly baked breads.
>
> If dining out was more your style, there were plenty of places to choose from: Peck's Restaurant, Daisy Ice Cream Shop, Franny Durkin's Tavern, Russ Richard's Tavern, Hilman's Chili Parlor, Schoenie's Chili Parlor and, of course, one of the biggest draws on the "Avenue," Coutrakon's Confectionary, affectionately nick-named "Couts."

Memorial Hospital

When you mention Memorial today you think of this ever-expanding medical complex that dominates the area north of Carpenter Street between 1st and 2nd Streets and beyond. It now employs thousands and is at the heart of the medical district that was carved out of one square mile on the northwest side of Springfield.

The hospital started out in 1897 as a modest, ill-thought out enterprise on 5th and North Grand in a spacious, two story Italianate mansion donated by a Dr. Langdon. The Springfield Hospital and Training School was formed by the Lutheran Missouri Synod without any public funding, originally to care for its Concordia Seminary students because "some local Lutheran leaders were dismayed that impressionable young men were in the care of Catholic nuns [at St. John's Hospital] who might or did seek to convert them" [p. 11, *Memorial Days: A History of Community Partnerships 1897—2007*].

However, within a generation the hospital grew into a community-wide North-End business with the early fears of its founders laid to rest. In fact, the by-laws of the institution were amended in 1931, changing the charter to a general non-denominational hospital, with the community assuming its operation and control. Since that time there has been a cooperative relationship, albeit sometimes tenuously so, with St. John's Hospital, which until this last decade had been the larger hospital.

For a little more of the backstory, the little hospital ran into financial difficulties from the start and by the time the Depression was in full swing (1931), it was in such serious trouble, bent on floundering, that a group of concerned citizens, including George W. Bunn and Robert C. Lanphier, assumed the debt and management duties. They then put in place a 27-person board that read like a Who's Who of Springfield (of which one-third were women, including Bertha Lanphier, wife of Robert Lanphier). That intervention stabilized the operation so well that by 1934 preliminary construction plans were drawn for a modern building that would support a needed second hospital.

In 1936 the building committee headed by Mr. Lanphier increased its expectations and felt that it could build a 200-bed hospital on seven floors (and with a nurses' home) for still less than a million dollars. In 1938 Mr. Lanphier again stepped up and donated $5000 for new X-Ray equipment in the present hospital. That same year the board formally announced plans for a 300-bed facility. Five months later, St. Johns, not to be undone and fearful of the intrusion, announced construction plans of its own: a $1.25 million addition that would make it, in the words of the *State Journal*, "the largest private hospital in the United States."

In June of 1941 a $1.1 million capital campaign commenced for Memorial and within a month nearly half of the goal was reached due to the eleemosynary spirit of four major donors. Alice Bunn, Mildred Bunn, Bertha Lanphier and Susan Bartholf gifted most of that money in the first 24 hours of the drive. Situated on four city blocks, Memorial Hospital of Springfield was dedicated in 1943 with an open house on September 26. When the public walked through the Art Deco entrance they were in awe of the hospital's seven stories intersecting at a 10-story central tower.

Most of the investment, including the $300,000 debt service, was paid off within two years thanks to the generosity of the public-spirited families with means. But perhaps the largest single support came from the local Masonic Order, which laid the hospital's cornerstone.

My mother actually worked as a registered nurse at the old hospital for a few months sometime after she left the Franciscan Order—it may have been around 1941. In 1950 Mom brought my sister and me to the new hospital for tonsillectomies. I vividly recall coming back there the night after the surgery due to hemorrhaging. My five-year-old self was terrified in the O.R. when what looked like space people cauterized my throat; I'll never forget looking up at this humongous bright light right overhead. For years afterwards I relived that terrible experience whenever Dad drove us past Memorial.

Coal Mines

Around 1900 Springfield had become a rapidly expanding city (population 34,000) with a strong and growing industrial base of 300 firms. Included in those were dozens of coal mines scattered around the city and surrounding areas. In fact, Sangamon County was the leading coal producer in the nation's leading coal state. Coal was discovered in Springfield in 1858, and Sangamon County had its first coal mine in 1866. The following year The Old North Mine was opened on the Henry Converse farm, north of the present Camp Lincoln. It became one of the largest producing mines in the county for many years.

On my mother's side of the family the Roscetti men were almost all coal miners. At our boisterous Italian family gatherings—holidays, weddings, as well as funerals—the men would talk about the tortuous years they spent eking out a living under ground, most of it as production work (tonnage per man per day). My grandfather, Bert Roscetti, worked at Peerless Mine, north of East Sangamon Avenue, when my mother was a child, around 1915. Two of my uncles and possibly Grandpa ended up at Peabody #10 by Kincaid, after the war years. A self-educated man ("I never saw a school teacher's face"), Grandpa was proud to have personally known United Mine Worker's famous leader John L. Lewis, who resided in Springfield for some years; he loved him like many people loved FDR. He would talk about him to me for hours on end.

Not only was the work relentlessly grueling, but dangerous as well. My mom's uncle, Alfonso Antonacci, a miner, died at 48 in 1938 from a heart attack. He left 11 children and a wife. Here is how my mom's cousin, Hugo, described the scene when they got home from the funeral, in his autobiography which I edited. It will give you a glimpse of what North-End pride meant in those days, even to immigrants.

> I remember the morning after we buried Pop. The lady across the street came to see Mom. She told Mom, "Mrs. Antonacci, take off your apron and get in the car with me." Mom asked, "Where we go?" in her broken English. The neighbor lady responded, "With all these kids and no husband, we are going to apply for aid to dependent children--you are entitled to it." Mom seemed genuinely

shocked at the notion and said, "No, I no go. I no go." The neighbor couldn't believe what she was hearing when Mom explained, "That's relief and relief is only for poor or sick people . . . and nobody in our family is poor or sick." The lady tried to reason with Mom, saying, "But how are you going to support eleven children with no husband?" Mom said, "The small children got older brothers and sisters and some are working and they'll take care of their younger brothers and sisters." [*The Life and Times of Hugo Antonacci,* 2006]

Several of Hugo's brothers likely quit school, possibly Lanphier, and went to the mines or other work the very next day. Hugo finishes the story by saying, "And we did. I was twenty-one at the time and worked as a clerk-steno in a local law office. We all pitched in and helped raise the family. No relief for Mom; she didn't think we were poor and needed it!" That same kind of pride carried Hugo throughout his life. He proudly told me he paid for his three children's college and master's degrees without ever considering getting scholarships or grants or loans. "We pay our own way," he told me.

When I was growing up, the only coal mine I can recollect that resembled a producing mine (it stopped in 1949, when I was five) was across from the cemetery on North Walnut as you headed out of town toward the airport. It was Panther Creek Mine #2. From Jim Krohe's map of Sangamon County mines in his authoritative little book packed with information, *Midnight at Noon: A History of Coal Mining in Sangamon County*, there were fifty-three coal mines during a 100-year period starting in 1869.

The *1989 Directory of Coal Mines in Illinois* shows that six mines were in the general North-End area during the first half of the twentieth century. It gives the last owners' names and periods of operation: Peabody Mine 59 (1930-1951); Lincoln Coal Company Empire Mine #1 (1928); Standard Coal Company (1926-1936); Cantrall Coal (1909-1915); Panther Creek (1929-1953); and Springfield Coal Company (1903-1911).

When I was a boy, there were remnants of the tipple of a mine just a few blocks north of Lanphier, at 11th and Ridgely. It was not far from the long-gone Rolling Mill factory that had been a major North-End employer in the early 1900s and before.

The coal industry was huge in and around Springfield in the first half of the 20th Century. If you ever saw a map of Springfield with mine runs superimposed, about the only area that was not catacombed with coal seams was the state capitol. When I walked to grade school at St. Al's I would walk right past an escape tunnel that had a vertical shaft exposed on the southeast corner of 19th and Ridgely. All that protected kids and unsuspecting drunks was a rickety wooden fence. Even though it was filled up years ago, the city likely prohibits ever building a house on that property.

Like myself, many Lanphier students had fathers and uncles and brothers and grandfathers working those mines in and around Springfield. Graduating students went into the mines even when I was in school, but that was a dwindling number. Even current Lanphier principal, Artie Doss, worked the mines for nine years before going into education.

Coal was king most of those years, and it was a major employer for many North-End breadwinners. One figure I saw at the library had it at 7,750 miners (and others connected with the industry) in Sangamon County (*1926 Coal Report*). The 1941 figures showed 2,839 mining personnel in Sangamon County. My guess is that the North-End miners likely numbered 1,000 or so during those periods, which made it a major employer along the lines of Pillsbury and Sangamo.

Each mine had large numbers of workers in three shifts, between 80 and 200, even up to 700. Even though a miner could conceivably earn $2000 a year in the '20s and '30s, Krohe points out that due to seasonal reductions, the terrible miners' wars in the 1930s, and other forced idleness resulted in annual incomes of between $600 and $1000. He quotes one miner in that period lamenting that "I put in 27 years in the underground coal mines, and I was never out of debt in those years."

Memorial Pool

The officially-named Soldiers and Sailors Memorial Pool had a slow start after being proposed before WWI. However, it got a big boost from the local chapter of the American Business Club when it launched the private fundraising project with a successful band concert in 1926. With the help of two mortgages from local banks, the pool opened ceremoniously on June 16, 1928, with Mr. and Mrs. Robert Lanphier's daughter, Margret, jumping in first, followed by hundreds of other children and then adults.

The pool was designed by local architects Helmle and Helmle in a two-pool concept—one side for adults and the other for children. There was a long brick bathhouse with lockers for 1,200 bathers. It was situated such that you had to enter it and take a shower and don sterilized suits before entering either pool. On the side of the entire bathhouse was an ornate pergola laden with plants that gave class and sophistication to the whole experience.

Although the admission price was modest (50 cents for adults and 25 cents for children), the Park District allowed 12,000 children free access in its first year. Although it provided much needed relief from the summer heat—Bunn Park's lagoon had been the only alternative— for many years, sadly, Memorial Pool closed down for good in 1974 due to shifting population centers around town plus deterioration of the facility.

Like many North-End kids, I spent many, many summer days at the pool. However, I had an inauspicious start as a swimmer when my dad took me there and told me, "Just step in." I did as he directed, but we were at the deep end and I went straight to the bottom. I coughed and gaged my way back up, gulping all the air I could when I emerged. I cried hysterically, so Dad took me home. Mom asked him how our first swimming lesson went. I looked at him, waiting for a response. He just shook his head and went into the front room and read the paper.

There were a number of other businesses and factories on the North End that would make for an even richer historical sketch of the area, if time and space would allow. If you are interested, *The Springfield Journal-Register*'s supplement on the North End ("Springfield North

End Revisited...a Celebration," May 5, 1984) has an excellent summary of twelve of them. Among them are the Reisch Brewery, Springfield Iron Works, and the Zoo Park.

Pillsbury Mills as it appeared in its heyday, circa 1950s. You get some idea of how expansive an operation it was. The C&IM railroad yard sits just behind it. Lanphier is just two blocks north west. [Courtesy of the Sangamon Valley Collection]

The International Shoe Company on the near north side of Springfield. c. 1940s [Courtesy Sangamon Valley Collection]

St. John's Hospital around 1887. Another wing was added to the left in 1891. This view was taken from Eighth and Mason looking northward. [Courtesy of Sangamon Valley Collection.]

Springfield Hospital & Training School on the corner of 5th and North Grand Ave. in 1903. The two wings flank the original Langdon mansion. The hospital retained this configuration into the 1930s. [Courtesy of Sangamon Valley Collection]

Panther Creek Mine #2 operated from 1928-1949. I remember it well as a young boy. It was just north of Yates Street and Route 29 (Walnut Street), just north of North Grand Avenue. Today, a dentist's office sits just south of the once majestic mine. [Courtesy Sangamon Valley Collection]

Steinkuehler's was a local grocery store on 11th Street and Reservoir, just north of the railroad tracks, one block south of Lanphier. Kids could run down there to grab a quick sandwich or candy over lunch break. My parents used to stop there to pay their light bill, get hunting licenses, car license, etc. 1967 [Courtesy Sangamon County Tax Assessor Office]

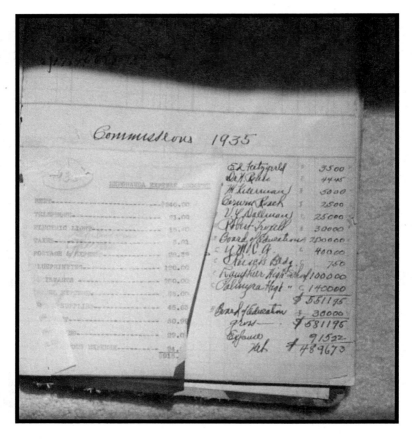

1935 Ledger from Bullard and Bullard Architects, showing the first entry for work rendered for the Lanphier High School project. The initial commission was $1000 (line 10, above), followed by two more entries in succeeding years: $2000 in 1936 and $1484.24 in 1937. There is another entry in the above ledger to the Board of Education plus two more in the next two years, so this firm was busy and profitable during the height of the Depression. [Courtesy Mrs. Eileen Bullard]

Chapter 8

The Lanphier High School Building

Much of the history I have written here is from personal interviews, going through all the *Lan-Hi* yearbooks, the Sangamon Valley Collection, files, and newspapers. You realize, of course, that school buildings themselves are also a source of information: they are privy to their own historical ebbs and flows, and this story is told in many ways by Lanphier's edifice herself. She has taught me a lot of her history just from listening to her and watching her the last three years teaching there. As I walk through her entrance and climb her stairs and head down her long halls substitute teaching, from time to time I hear her gently whispering her secret stories to me. And I smile. Then later, I write them down for you to read. So with her help also, I wrote this history—in large part, her history.

The December 22, 1935 *Springfield Journal* carried an article about the proposed high school next to two drawings of it. Designed by Springfield architects Carl T. Meyer and Clark W. Bullard, it was to cost $300,000 (almost half of the school district's annual budget) and partially funded with P.W.A. funds (Public Works Administration, not to be confused with the W.P.A., Roosevelt's Works Progress Administration). Here are parts of that article.

The main entrance will be on Eleventh Street. A wing of the building with an entrance on North Grand avenue…is the gymnasium, which will accommodate 1,000 students in physical education classes. The gymnasium will seat 2,000 spectators.

The auditorium, seating 600 students, extends back of the main building. Entrance to the auditorium is gained by going in the Eleventh street door, up a flight of stairs and across a hall. The auditorium will be equipped with a stage and dressing rooms and is expected to be utilized not only for student assemblies but for literary, dramatic and theatrical presentations

On the ground floor beneath the auditorium will be a cafeteria, seating 300 students. The room will also be used as a study hall. Also on the ground floor will be the industrial arts department, with shops for several types of industrial activity, including sheet metal work, elementary electricity, woodwork and pre-vocational activities. To the left of the entrance on the ground floor will be rooms for domestic science classes.

A well-equipped library will be on the first floor, together with several academic class rooms. General offices of administration will be located to the left of the main entrance on the first floor.

Besides regular class rooms, the second floor will have a special music room, speech room and textile and cooking class rooms. The chemistry and physics laboratories will be on the second floor. A public address system is being planned so that the principal may talk to all the pupils in their respective class rooms at the same time.

Radios will be installed so that programs of an educational nature may be received.

The exterior of the building will be finished in brick of a color to be chosen by the board of education. A name for the school likewise will be selected by the board. [The exterior brick chosen was common red while the interior brick work was blond.]

What strikes me every time I pass by my old alma mater are the bold aluminum art deco letters that spell out "Lanphier High School" over the main entrance. For some reason that lettering style jumps out at me as if to say, "Remember me? I'm still here!"

Bids were opened on January 2, 1936, and construction commenced in early spring. The brand new edifice was completed on schedule just 12 months later in record time for the first class (coming from Converse High School) of 1937 to graduate that May. "Everything that could be moved from the old Converse School was carried over to the new structure by the students, the faculty, and the principal. The moving was done on Saturday, and classes were resumed at Lanphier on Monday, January 25; and has been in session ever since" [1954 *Lan-Hi*, p.10]. That first year's full enrollment was 748 students.

The evening of the first day of school the student body and the public enjoyed the opening of the new gym. Now called the Lanphier Lions, the basketball team was victorious over Pleasant Plains with the score 36-20. The gym was packed to its 2,000 seating capacity. Among the roaring crowd were Mr. Robert C. Lanphier's brother and sister-in-law, Mr. and Mrs. Goin Lanphier.

On April 1, 1937, the official dedication was held in the gymnasium packed with 2,000 parents, neighbors and dignitaries. Mr. Lanphier himself proudly whispered some brief remarks of appreciation and then was presented with a large framed photograph of his likeness which was placed above the front entrance where it is still today. (He passed away two years after the school that bears his name was dedicated.)

Like most building proposals, the finished school was not exactly like the plans laid out above in the newspaper article. For one thing, the planned auditorium on the east side of the structure was not built; instead a stage on the north side of the gym took on the auditorium's various functions. Also, the labs were on the south end of the third floor when I was there, not the second floor. The school ended up having nine classrooms, five laboratories and twelve special rooms for a final cost of $315,000.

Principal George Stickney would try to mold the new school into the ideal he had in mind from the start. "He came with the dream of building an up-to-date high school that would be advantageous to all students from the north end. During his years…he made his dream into a reality. Lanphier High was always thought of as 'his school'" [1987 *Lan-Hi,* p. 50]

Construction picture of the front of the new school by Bullard & Bullard Architects. Actually, the school building was a joint effort of two architect firms, Carl T. Meyer and Clark W. Bullard's—possibly to spread the work around in the Depression era. The mound of dirt in the background is the last of the reservoir. [Courtesy of Mrs. Eileen Bullard]

The construction project No. 1573 is nearing completion in the fall of 1936. Here you see the back of the school where they are putting finishing touches on the boiler room roof. Note the trees in the foreground that once lined the Park lagoons. [Courtesy of Mrs. Eileen Bullard]

Architect's picture of Lanphier's finished lobby. It was taken from the south side hallway to the north first floor hallway. The crossed-stars logo dominates the floor today as it did on the first day of school, Monday, January 25, 1937. [Courtesy of Mrs. Eileen Bullard]

Architect's picture of the finished gymnasium. Note in the lower right it mentions the name of Alzina Construction Co. as the principle contractor. [Courtesy of Mrs. Eileen Bullard]

The basement of Lanphier is accessed by meandering around the boiler room and two short flights of stairs. Containing a huge water heater, washers and driers, it was the room sometimes used by Coach Ransford during some of his wrestling practices when I was in school. Few students have probably ever seen it. [*Lan-Hi's* Katie Fitzgerald]]

The dedication plaque hangs on the south wall just off the lobby. [Lan-Hi's Katie Fitzgerald]

Chapter 9

LHS's Formative Years—The Thirties

I was delighted to see that my aunt Claudia Roscetti Klameier was among the first students to graduate from Lanphier. The first *Lan-Hi* had her as "Home Ec[onomics] 2" and under her picture was a couplet celebrating her stature: "'Tis better to be small and shine/Than to be big and cast a shadow."

Dad told me more than once that "those Dago girls were really good looking but their brothers wouldn't let us take 'em out." Notwithstanding his slang (which my Italian side of the family never took issue with), Dad was right. But in the end he did get to go out with a beautiful Italian lady, my mom. (Read about their courtship in my book *Sister Raphael: The Personal and Family History of Jennie Roscetti Mitchell*.) As I went from page to page in that first yearbook I kept coming across Italian girls who *were* really quite beautiful: girls such as Celia Frasco, Jean Iocca, Jennie Vespa and Rose Vicaio.

Celia Antonacci-Frasco Ackerman ('37) was my mom's first cousin and my oldest Lanphier interviewee. She told me recently that when she came over for her senior year, her first impression was that "the new school was so big and roomy compared to Converse." Celia's dad died young and her mom (my grandmother's sister) married a widower with six young children. My mother used to tell me how hard her aunt had it raising his kids plus her own four. Celia had to rush home on Black Avenue and help her mom with the chores so "I had no social life at school. I didn't enjoy high school also because of the stress of helping Mom. Plus, neither she nor my stepfather knew how to read or write, so I struggled in school." As soon as she graduated with that first class in May, she got a waitress job uptown.

Those May 1937 seniors, headed by senior class president John Fults, numbered 76 with 23 of them having transferred from SHS and other area schools. Their class carried with it a safe motto: "You Receive from Life What You Put into It." The junior class's president, Harold Reich, praised his 120 classmates by reminiscing, "…then freshmen walked into 'Dear Old Converse" in September of the year 1934. Their knees shaking in anticipation and rather perplexed smiles on their faces the Junior Class. [They] enjoyed three years of school in Converse and [then] Lanphier." The sophomore class had about the same number as the juniors, while the freshman class totaled 180. The first graduate of Lanphier was Joe Allison (May '37) because of alphabetical order.

There were a surprising number of clubs and organizations. I suppose they were started while at Converse. We had an orchestra from the beginning (although it didn't last too many years). Among the 16 groups were band, choir, student council (Bob Griffin, president), Commercial Club and Quill & Scroll.

The new school newspaper was christened the *Lanphier Light* (with the motto "It Shall Burn As A Beacon Ever Beckoning Youth To Truth," later editors lopping off the first four words) by its inaugural staff. The first volume of the *Lan-Hi* explained the bi-weekly transition from Converse High School to LHS this way: "The first Journalism Class, Press Club and Quill & Scroll was organized in January 1937. This group [juniors and seniors] put out the final edition of the *Script*, the old Converse High mimeographed paper. Now all issues of the *Lanphier Light* [will have] 4-8 pages [as] printed news sheets."

The first senior class play at the new school was "Charley's Comedy," the adventures and misadventures of three college chums. The old farcical comedy was presented on the night of April 29, 1937.

The only teacher's name I recognized that first year was Mr. Cleo Dopp, a social studies instructor, who was likely a founding faculty member of Converse High School, so he was probably the longest serving teacher up through 1962, when I graduated. One of his early students gave up their decades-old secret of how to get Mr. Dopp off topic: "All you had to do was mention Michigan and its sports program and he would go into heartfelt detail about his alma mater. It worked every time."

The second year (1937-1938) Rolla Sorrells appeared as the football coach. Miss Ethel Furlich started in 1938 as the Latin teacher. One of her early students told me fate allowed Miss Furlich to catch the last ship from Europe before the Germans blockaded passenger ships. Mr. Hoffman joined Sorrells and Dopp in the social studies department in 1939, along with Esther Duncan, the Lanphier music department's second director. Miss Helen Jeske came in 1940 as a P.E. teacher.

The very next year after her arrival, Miss Duncan's choral group won the national choral contest in Flint, Michigan. Her groups had done well over the years, even into my era. However, after her win in Flint, she was not allowed to attend the national contests again until after the war years.

Principal Stickney and Dean of Boys Lee Goby were an effective disciplinary team from the start, as several of the early students confirmed to me. Mr. Stickney was a short stocky man ("built like a tank") who had been a competitive wrestler in school. If he saw a student running down the hall, one student recalled, he would sometimes hold out his arm tightly and the student would more often than not flip over it and hit the ground, in which case the sin was indeed its own punishment.

Mr. Goby used another tactic which also worked effectively. When an offending boy came to his office, the Dean of Boys would close the door, mete out the punishment—invariably with a paddle—and the student, now repentant, would apologize to him on his way out. Years later, Dorothy Boehner, school secretary, describing Mr. Goby's toughness, said many a day she would hear the varied excuses tardy students would try out on him (e.g. train on tracks) to no avail. He continued to "crack problem cases," as one student described Mr. Goby's method, for several more years.

Here's how one student from that early era described the two men:

> Mr. Stickney was a quiet man, seemed sort of a sourpuss to me because he hardly ever smiled. But he seemed to be an effective administrator. I remember how he would station himself in the middle of the lobby with his hands behind his back and monitor the flow of students at the beginning of the school day and between classes. He looked down the north hall and then the south hall and you better not be seen by him after that first bell rang or he would hand you a tardy slip. One day I was late and he caught me and I coolly explained that I was going to the office to make an announcement. I said over the PA system that our after-school club meeting was cancelled. I did that more than once and he never caught on to me.
>
> Mr. Goby portrayed himself as a stern man with an authoritative air. But inside he was really a good guy who didn't easily get ruffled. Sometimes when we were eating lunch in the bleachers, he would come up and make sure all was well. As he was leaving our area some kid would holler out, "It's all off!" Another would say, "What's all off?" and several would answer, "Goby's hair." He was bald but that kind of behind his back ribbing never fazed him.

Lanphier students have seen several major upgrades to our school over the years, the first one proposed the very next year after it opened. It's not clear why it wasn't constructed at the start, but the school board spent another $60,000 on this project (which I'll call the north wing) starting in 1939. Even though the P.W.A. underwrote 47 percent of the cost, the balance the school board paid out was still a boatload of money in those days. A local architect recently surmised that complete funding had probably not been available from the start, so the wing was budgeted in a subsequent fiscal year.

Several newspaper articles at the time told of a contentious battle among the school board members as to whether they should even have an addition so soon after the new building was completed. One meeting got so heated that three members resigned. Beginning in September of 1938, the addition idea was dropped by the board, a few days later revived, and the next week it was debated again and passed. It's anybody's guess what all the infighting was about. My guess is that tempers flared because of countervailing views on how to spend limited dollars. Remember, we had been in the grips of the Great Depression for a decade.

In the 1940-41 year book, there is a before-and-after picture of the two-story addition, which seamlessly integrated with the main structure, wrapping around it on the north side. Along with eight classrooms upstairs, it held the first floor cafeteria/lunch room (which doubled as a study hall) and a band room.

The Lanphier Light

It Shall Burn As A Beacon Ever Beckoning Youth To Truth

| Volume I | SPRINGFIELD, ILLINOIS, THURSDAY, APRIL 1, 1937 | Number 4 |

G. E. STICKNEY RELATES DEVELOPMENT OF SCHOOL THRU LAST SEVEN YEARS

Parent Teachers Association

By Max Worney

SEAT OF LEARNING NOW LOCATED WHERE ONCE THE CITY WATER WORKS STOOD

Lanphier Boosters Club

By Russell Hatten

Congratulations Lanphier

Lanphier Choir Win Sub-Division Title

Modern Equipment Welcomed By All Science Classes

One of the first Lanphier newspapers [Courtesy Randy Miller ('71), LHS historian and archivist; LHS Hall of Fame inductee, 2012]

This is the six-inch refractor telescope from the Watch Factory observatory. It appears to be from the 1930s, so it replaced the original 8-1/4 inch from the early 1900s.It was donated to the Boy Scouts of Springfield in 1962 by Frederick Carl Holtz, former VP and Chief Engineer and Director of Sangamo. It had been in storage for some years before Mr. Holtz gave it to the Scouts' Camp Bunn. [Ken Mitchell]

The North Wing addition to Lanphier's original building was approved in the fall of 1938. It was likely built so soon after the construction of the new school due to budget constraints in previous years. It was completed for the school year 1940-1941 and included a band room, a cafeteria and classrooms.
[1941 *Lan-Hi*]

The Gold Star plaque, honoring those Lanphier students who died in WWII, hangs proudly in the main lobby. [Photography Class' Cassidy Johnson]

Chapter 10

The War Decade—The Forties

There were rumblings of war from 1935 onward, but the European conflict became a stark reality on September 1, 1939 when Hitler's armies rolled over Poland. Americans wanted no part of another European war but got pushed into it anyway on December 7, 1941. From 12:48 p.m. through most of that Sunday afternoon, Americans were glued to their radios when the news of Pearl Harbor hit the airwaves. There would be no "normal" for the next three years and nine months for every American household and for every Lanphier student.

The rest of the 1940-1941 school year was spent wondering how long the war would last and if the senior boys would be following their graduated classmates into the recruiting stations.

The school tried its best to run a normal operation. Most clubs and sports kept up their routines, but the *Lan-Hi* staff reflected the country's mood by dedicating the 1942 yearbook to "Our Men in the Service." At that time (spring 1942) approximately 80 graduates and former students had joined the armed services. All the soldiers were again remembered in the following year's *Lan-Hi* dedicated it "To Those Who Serve."

The seventh volume of the yearbook (1943 *Lan-Hi*) announced the hiring of Ted Boyle to the faculty as its new math teacher. The following year he was the baseball coach. He was lucky to have a 17-year-old outfielder on his team who hustled like crazy to catch every ball. Robin Evan Roberts would one day join that rare breed of athlete into the Baseball Hall of Fame as a pitcher. In the 1944 *Lan-Hi*, however, he was focusing on other sports: "Evan shines as a leader in basketball and football." Mr. Sorrells bragged to us in my Econ class that he coached the famous athlete; what he forgot to mention (or I forgot) was that was on the basketball court.

Art Spiegel ('46) scrimmaged as a sophomore against Roberts and the other senior basketball teammates and stayed friends with him throughout his life. Here's Art's personal impression of our most famous alumnus:

> Evan was a mentor kind of guy who would take kids under his wing. He was a serious student as well as an excellent athlete. He was nice to everybody…a real gentleman and he never swore or used bad language. He was cool and level headed, but very competitive and aggressive when he played sports. He didn't like his first name and would tell you so if you called him by "Robin." He was the Jack Armstrong [i.e. the all-American boy] type of guy whom everyone respected. And he remained that way even after he became a baseball hero. He would come back to some of our reunions and was the same old Evan we knew at Lanphier.

Curious why he was noted more for his football and basketball skill in high school and even college, I asked Art how he turned into a superstar pitcher in the Majors:

Evan got a basketball scholarship to Michigan State and won the Silver Trophy there, which signified he was the best basketball player on the team during his college years. But I suspect the Big Leagues scouted him during the baseball seasons and saw his potential as a pitcher. He wasn't a flashy pitcher but had great control. They were right because as a senior he was one of the first pitchers drafted and signed with the Phillies in 1948. To show you what kind of fellow Evan was, he used some of his signing bonus [$25,000] to build his folks a nice house here in Springfield.

Fresh out of Kansas State and Michigan, Miss Norton was the newest member of the English Department, in the fall of 1943. Mildred Norton was one of my favorite teachers, one who taught us not only English but many life lessons.

The Golden Anniversary yearbook describes one change at Lanphier during the war years: "In 1943, courses pertaining to the war were included in the curriculum. One of the classes offered was a preflight course. This class helped several of the graduating seniors who planned to serve in a branch of the service. Many of the students who took advantage of these courses passed their cadet aviation examinations."

The Langfelder Odyssey

Ossie Langfelder ('44), past mayor of Springfield and member of the LHS Hall of Fame, was just 14 when he entered Lanphier as a sophomore in 1941. As he recounts in his riveting memoir, *My Incredible Journey*, he and his family had fled Austria's Nazi occupation in 1939. He learned some English while in England but had a difficult time adjusting to his new school in Springfield. Here is a recollection from his book:

> I enjoyed attending Lanphier High School, although I was only allowed to attend dances if [my sister] Edith and her girlfriends accompanied me. Since I was rather scrawny, I was never active in sports, and even Mr. Rake, our gym instructor, threw me out of class. He was a very crude, cursing individual whom, I felt, didn't like anyone who spoke to him in a polite manner.

Ossie told me that when he was dismissed from P.E., Mr. Rake thought he was hurting him. In fact, Ossie, whose offense was not being able to climb the rope to the gym ceiling, was delighted to avoid that class, which was normally a graduation requirement.

Ossie continued the story about his time at Lanphier by discussing what the war meant to the students:

> The Japanese attacked Pearl Harbor as I was completing my first semester at Lanphier. The war, at first, had a minor impact on the student body, but as we progressed into our senior year, all the young male students, upon reaching the age of seventeen, enlisted in the armed services. Unbeknownst to my parents, with the help of...Mr. Stickney, I also attempted to enlist, but to no avail.

Ossie explained to me that in order to enlist at seventeen you had to be a U.S. citizen. After he graduated in the January 1944 class and turned eighteen, he was drafted. He was anxious to serve in Europe, so he could go back home. Instead, he spent his service time in the South Pacific.

He also related a story to me that was not in his book. Several teachers—Mr. Sach, Mr. Gerald and Mr. McCall, in particular—took him under their wing and made his transition more comfortable. In particular, Mr. McCall had Ossie help him make bread boxes in his woodworking class. Part of the war effort precluded bakers from slicing bread and so Mr. McCall's "invention," as Ossie called it, made it easy for parents to slice the bread within the confines of the boxes by using a metal channel device.

With Hitler's defeat in May, 1945, and the Japanese surrender the following August, current Lanphier students could breathe a sigh of relief and return to the normalcy of school life at school that fall.

When I asked Donna Cornish Krueger ('46) how many were in her graduating class she responded:

> I want to say around 226 were in the 1946 class, but I can't be sure. I could count the number of senior pictures in my yearbook, but you have to remember that only about two-thirds who started actually graduated. Twenty five or so of our men quit to join the service and those who returned weren't all from our class.

The other factor Donna mentioned in our conversation relating to graduation numbers was that quite a few students quit when they were sixteen to join the work force. It was not common until the '50s that most students finished their high school educations. And as in the case of my father, some students didn't even start high school, although that pretty much ended with the previous generation.

Remembrances from the '40s

During our time together, Donna thought back on her Lanphier days and related some interesting stories that popped into her mind. She said that long-time secretary Dorothy Boehner started in that position while Donna was in school. (Ms. Boehner was the go-to person at Lanphier for close to 50 years. Coach Gardner laughed when I mentioned her name: "Whenever I needed something, all I would have to do is see Dot and she'd get it for me.") [Read more on Mrs. Boehner in Chapter 15.] Donna also recalled her classmate Claude Sowle as "the class clown. He was a real cutup." (Dr. Sowle later gained fame as the dean of Cincinnati Law School and other education posts and was a first round pick for Lanphier's first Hall of Fame inductees.)

She also spoke highly of one of her classmate's athleticism. Eleanor "Ruddy" Rudolph became a professional softball player for Caterpillar Tractor Company in a Peoria professional league—likely the first Lanphier female athlete to achieve such renown, years before female athletics was realized there. Another staff person she praised was long-serving school librarian, Nella Hughes: "She was so helpful with my assignments and always told me, 'Here's what you need.' There are some people you always remember."

One of the most interesting Lanphier stories surrounds "the infamous class of '48." Art Spiegel just happened to think of it in our second sit-down interview and I'm glad he did.

> We had some really smart kids at Lanphier, but we don't get credit for that distinction because it usually is saved for Springfield High. Some were brilliant, like Herbie Kochman and Bill Porter and Keith Goodwin. But we were common people and so their achievements weren't recognized as much.
>
> Anyway, in '48 somebody got hold of the test in English class, I think, and everybody got A's. Some of the top kids were in that class [not the three mentioned above], but they didn't take into account the bell shaped curve. The teacher asked who got the test and not a single soul in class would rat the person out. So it was decided that that year there would be no one admitted into National Honor Society, inside or outside of that English class. Can you believe it? Nobody caved, even then.

One of the most fun couples I met as I interviewed Lanphier alums was the Kloppenburgs. Henry or "Bud" ('44) was in some classes with Charliene Tucker ('45). Here's the sweet story of how Charliene recalls the beginning of their courtship:

I was sixteen and Henry decided he wanted to ask me out. So he comes up to me after class and says, "How would you like to go tobogganing with me sometime?" to which I agreed since he seemed like a nice young man. Well, he didn't have a toboggan at the time and so he began construction on it. It took him weeks and he kept telling me it would be done soon. (There were no phones during the war so we had to communicate at school.) When he finally did finish it, there was no snow and we had to wait and wait. Finally, Henry said, "Let's just go to a show at the Orpheum." That night it snowed and snowed so we had trouble getting a cab uptown. Finally we were able to get a bus and had our first date. We never did go tobogganing.

Henry related a heartwarming story about an act of kindness displayed by two of his teachers. He came down with a blood clot in his leg, and he had to have complete bed rest for eight weeks. Miss Furlich and Miss Freund would visit him daily, first at the hospital and later at his home, and go over his lessons with him. Had it not been for their going the extra mile, he would have had to repeat that entire semester.

Charliene was an excellent student and was in National Honor Society *and* elected senior class president, a rare feat during those male-dominated days. [Read Charliene's speech to the NHS years later, in the Appendix.] (She told me something I did not know: During the early days of Lanphier, women teachers in Springfield would not be hired back once they got married, on the theory that they would be taking another family's job.) Charliene was also on the *Light* staff and had a column called "Snooping Elda," in which she would report who was dating whom and breakups and other tidbits that she "overheard" in the halls. No one on staff, except the advisor, knew that it was Charliene's column, since she used her middle name. Here's an example from the June 7, 1945 newspaper, where "Elda" surveys students about what they do on Saturday nights:

John Ingram—"Oh, my girl and I usually take in a show, walk out to her girlfriend's house, and then we take the long way home." Then someone added, "He's just dreaming. He sits home and bites his fingernails."

Death of a Student

The Kloppenburgs relayed a sad story about a student drowning at Lake Springfield during the 1946 Junior Class picnic in early June. All-star student athlete Bob Cain's brother, Doug, was calling for help after being exhausted from trying to retrieve an oar from a boat two Lanphier couples were riding in. His friend, Gene Stevenson, jumped in to rescue his friend but after getting a life preserver to him, he drowned trying to get back while fighting the waves. Gene was a popular 16-year-old junior active in the a cappella choir and a regular on the basketball team. There was a plaque placed in the front lobby dedicated to Gene; on it is the Biblical quote "Greater love hath no man than to lay down his life for his friend." Miss Duncan had her choral group sing at his funeral.

That plaque still resides on the south wall of the main lobby near one listing Gold Star WWII former students. (Does anyone ever look at them and wonder who these students were, or are they too busy growing up?) Are there other Lanphier students or alumni who had been killed in the subsequent conflicts and wars whom we don't know about? One of my classmates, Glen King, was killed in Vietnam. [See the Gold Star list in the Appendix.] In the first floor south hall there is a row of picture frames with almost 700 alphabetized names of all Lanphier students who served in World War II. This "Honor Roll" has gold stars next to the 18 men who sacrificed their lives for our country.

Key Club Begins

A significant addition to Lanphier's organizations was the Key Club, which made its appearance in 1948. A Kiwanis-sponsored high school boys group, Key Club was formed in Sacramento, California in 1925, just 10 years after Kiwanis itself began. As the name implies, it was chartered for key boys in the high schools to help in civic projects through initiative and leadership and lots of hard work. At first it was restricted to junior and senior boys who had displayed good citizenship and maintained a B-average. There were many activities Key Clubbers undertook at Lanphier, making it one of the most distinguished of the school's organizations. Under the leadership of Mr. Goby and Mr. Taylor, Key Club had 37 members within two years.

Also, in 1948, the north wing needed the room used for band practice, and so a one-story dedicated Band Room was added to the east end of the wing, where it is appreciated by aspiring musicians to this day.

A man I substitute-teach with sometimes turned out to be a fellow Lanphier alum. Phil Martin ('49), a very interesting and vivacious man who taught art for many years in Taylorville, mentioned a few things about Lanphier and his time there:

> Jack Beechler was a classmate of mine and a real sharp guy. Jack once dated 43 girls in 30 days [on a dare]…Later in life he paid for minted silver Lanphier coins and gave them to every one of our reunion returnees a few years back…
>
> Ms. Duncan taught us respect for teachers, students and the school. She had the most school spirit of any one I knew…It was tough to get in her a capella group—which carried a lot of prestige— and getting into senior choir wasn't too easy either…
>
> Miss Mable Kitch was my art teacher and, along with Casius Armstrong and Ms. Freund, was among my favorite teachers. Miss Kitch was the best; every Friday she would read *Gabriel and the Hour Book* to us in ninth grade. That little book, now all but forgotten, should be required reading; it's about right livelihood and morals. *Lanphier was more than a school—it taught us about life.*

At the beginning of the 1949 football season, Lanphier's team was able to play in the newly completed Memorial Stadium. Fans sat on bleachers (some from the old gymnasium of Springfield High School) and read the scores from the new scoreboard donated by the Elks Club. It would be used by all city high school teams for both football and track & field activities for many years. Dedicated on May 22, 1949 by school board president Robert C. Lanphier II— son of the man whose name was given to LHS— it was built between the practice field east of the school and the baseball stadium. Dave Beard ('53) told me he was a freshman and sat on those bleachers during that first season with a new stadium. "I think we used to play our football games at the Lanphier baseball park. But when we got that new field we really strutted our stuff, especially around the Springfield High crowd, our chief rival in all high school sports."

Dave Beatty ('46) was always interested in photography and for years he was Lanphier's official photographer for the senior class group picture. He was so good at photography that the school allowed him to take activity pictures while a student. He worked for the local paper starting in 1944 and continued to take pictures at Lanphier until 1963 when his photography business took off. He eventually earned the peer-designated Master Photographer in 1975, one of only two in Springfield. Dave was honored a couple of years ago when he was inducted into Lanphier's Hall of Fame. He told me he was twice honored because in addition to the HOF, he was given the opportunity of telling the senior class in his acceptance speech how they should bring the Lord into their lives to do really well while here on earth. Here's how he remembered his Lanphier days:

> I came to Lanphier in '43 after two
> and a half years at another school. It was a
> great move for me. I really enjoyed the school
> and the people. They let me do what I knew

how to do in photography. It was a real difference: they were more my kind of people at Lanphier

In the same vein Art Spiegel waxed nostalgic about his time at Lanphier in one of the most poignant tributes I have heard:

> Our teachers were all very good and treated us with respect. Our fellow students were for the most part great kids. I'm still good friends with many of them yet today. Some of us in the LHS Alumni Association are like brothers and sisters even though I went to school with them for only three years. We had a spirit at Lanphier: all for one and one for all. It was really that strong a bond.
>
> I had the advantage of attending Springfield High my first year. It was a nice school too but there were cliques there with varying social echelons. Lanphier was a cohesive student body. There was nobody there who thought they were better than anybody else. Sure, some kids were more popular because of sports or grades or singing, but I had the comfortable feeling that I wasn't out of place. When I came over, it was not hard to make friends. And there was no fighting. It was a nice place to go to school. *Lanphier was one of the best things that ever happened to me.*

Youth Drowns While Aiding Friend In Lake Springfield

A boating party for four Lanphier High school students ended in tragedy yesterday afternoon when one of the group, Eugene Stevenson, 16, son of Mr. and Mrs. Earl Stevenson, of 1921 North Ninth street, drowned in Lake Springfield as he aided one of his friends who had become exhausted while swimming.

Stevenson drowned as he sought to retrieve his life preserver which had broken away from him as he had thrown one to his friend, Douglas Cain, 16, of 2061 North Seventh street. The tragedy occurred about 4:20 p. m. approximately 75 yards off the east shore line of the lake, southeast of the Lindsay bridge.

The search for the body continued early today (Saturday). No diving had been attempted as divers declared it was too hazardous, the water being about 40 feet

EUGENE STEVENSON.

Front page story of the shocking death of LHS junior Gene Stevenson. The popular student would have graduated in 1947 had his life not been cut short by his selfless act of saving the life of Doug Cain. [*The Illinois State Journal,* June 8, 1946]

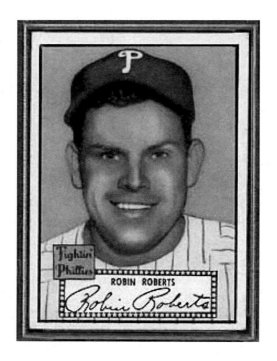

The greatest sports figure ever to come out of Springfield.
Robin Evan Roberts was one of our own—a North Ender and
a Lanphier graduate, class of '44. This Topps Baseball Card
#59 was from 1952, the year he won the most games in his
Major League career-28.

Arial view of the 24-acres that formerly made up Reservoir Park. It shows a late 1950s' photo of the newly completed Thomas Edison Junior High School, Lanphier Senior High School, its practice field, Memorial Field, and Lanphier Ball Park. The footprint of the main building is about the same as that of the reservoir it replaced. [Courtesy of Sangamon Valley Collection]

Chapter 11

The 1950s

Several of my favorite teachers came aboard in the 1950s. First was Orell Vanderwater, my biology teacher, arriving in 1950. Mr. Milton Dirst, fresh out of University of Illinois, taught chemistry and physics, starting in 1952. That same school year Mrs. Jo Oblinger, armed with a law degree, a young son and an FBI husband, Wally, started her long Lanphier career teaching business and government.

In 1953, three more top staff members pulled up to Lanphier and began long, distinguished careers. Arlyn Lober was hired to teach math and coach; Lester Brooks taught commercial classes as well as counseled boys; and Ed Ransford was hired as the Athletic Director, coach and P.E. teacher. I knew all three men as a student and to some degree as an adult. Interestingly, all three were members of what Tom Brokaw called The Greatest Generation—men who fought in the Second World War. Mr. Lober was a tank commander in Patton's Third Army. Mr. Ransford was a bomber copilot, dropping ordnance over Germany. Mr. Brooks worked as an aide-de-camp for both General Eisenhower and General Marshall and possibly also did a stint in the intelligence service.

During our interview, Arlyn quipped that he used to tell his friend Ed, that "at least you had dry barracks, warm meals and hot showers." When he would tell Ed "you probably were flying over us guys lots of times," Ed responded with a hand gesture mimicking an airplane banking and said in a deep affected voice, "And there we were at thirty-thousand…" and laughed. Like his fellow soldiers, that's about all I got out of Arlyn about the war, which had interrupted his and many others' college days.

Mid-term graduations, common in the past decades, were eliminated in Springfield public schools after the Senior Mid-Term graduation of January, 1954, according to Phil Shadid in his wonderful online blog "Springfield Converse High School 'Corsairs,'" which can be seen at www.illinoishsglorydays.com/id583.html. The likely reason for having mid-year graduations was to even out the age differences by having children on both sides of the September cut-off graduate in the same year. Students from that era told me that there was a strong line between the two classes, almost like the separation between grades.

Because of increased enrollment in 1954, Principal Stickney brought on board a young science teacher and coach from Springfield High, Mr. Petefish, as Assistant Principal. A Kiwanian himself, he took over as Key Club advisor and maintained that role through my time there and afterwards. Mr. Brooks took over the job of Dean of Boys at the same time.

On the 20th anniversary of Lanphier's founding, Principal Stickney—called "Gus" by many of his students, perhaps not to his face— was honored in the gymnasium with a tribute program for his impending retirement from principal as well. He was presented with a color oil portrait of himself painted by Mrs. Grace Woodruff, to be hung in the school building. Today you can see him still looking down on those students who are coming up and down the main staircase, along with the other principals, just above the awards and trophy cases that line the landing.

Thus, the first major administrative change occurred in the spring of 1957. Mr. Stickney, who had been long identified with Lanphier in the eyes of the students and the public, retired after 20 years as its principal plus three more years as the principal of Converse High School. Charles Petefish was the obvious choice as successor, as he and Lester Brooks worked well together.

After his tenure at Lanphier, Mr. Stickney accepted the post of Director of Secondary Education at District #186, where he organized the junior high school program, which changed the character of Lanphier the following year by making it a senior high school (with the addition of Edison Junior High School next door). He held the position of Assistant Superintendent of Schools for the last three years of his career. He retired in 1961 and left Springfield. He passed away five years later.

Mr. Petefish—"Pete" to his close friends and colleagues—was born on a farm near Carpenter Park (which bears his mother's family name) and then moved to Ashland. He began his career at Westchester High School as a coach and science teacher and then as freshman athletic coach and biology instructor at Springfield High School, where he stayed until appointed principal at Lanphier.

There were two additions to the building during this time period. In 1957 the boiler room, on the north side of the south wing of the school, was pushed out about twenty feet to house two new boilers. Why Lanphier needed a new power plant so soon was likely due to converting the heating system to natural gas. At the same time, more space was added to the back of the south end of the main building, where two of the vocational education classrooms were located, just next to the boiler room and at a right angle to it.

When I was in school we sometimes went down into the basement area (through the boiler room) after school to watch Coach Ransford wrestle with the heavyweight boys. In his mid-thirties he could still hold his own against such brutes as Henry Hackett and Mike Gabriel. I was impressed that he could take down—and sometimes keep down—these strapping boys half his age. When I recalled that with him years later (when his wife was in Mom's nursing home), he just smiled that big old smile of his and laughed.

Remembrances of the '50

Phil Shadid ('57) told me a funny story about the time Ted Boyle caught up with him and asked him about playing baseball. Always on the outlook for good players, Mr. Boyle stopped Phil as he was leaving his math classroom at the start of school. Here's how the conversation went:

"Phil, your brother was a heck of a pitcher [referring to Woody Shadid ('40)]. Can you pitch?"

"Not really, Mr. Boyle, but I can catch pretty well. But I'm not much of a hitter."

Phil told me that Mr. Boyle walked away and he never talked to Phil about joining the baseball team again. Phil laughed and said to me, "I'll never forget that story. It just struck me as funny."

Dave Dalbey ('58) remembers his time in the Hi-Y Club, which was sponsored by the YMCA. Joe Hoffman was its advisor. Dave said everybody called Mr. Hoffman "Comrade Joe" because he was such an adamant anti-Communist when teaching history. (When I went to school in the early sixties, we called him "Commie Joe.") One night Mr. Hoffman called Dave at his home and asked him if he wanted to attend the national convention of Hi-Y Clubs in Oxford, Ohio. Dave said another boy had bowed out and they needed a replacement. He agreed and Mr. Hoffman drove Dave and the other boys there. Dave said that was one of his best memories of Lanphier: "I had never been to something like that. It was great, talking to kids from all over the country about Christian youth programs."

Mr. Dopp was still susceptible to getting off-topic when a wise-guy student would bait him by mentioning the University of Michigan and its football team. (Remember in the Chapter on the Thirties, when they played that same trick on him?) Phil Shadid said, "Mr. Dopp would fall for that every time and when the hour was over he would say, 'Well, kids, we'll just have to get to that lesson tomorrow.'" Phil also remembered that Mr. Dopp, an economics teacher, was ahead of his time about his views of the political instability in the Arab countries. He emphasized to his classes during this period that there would be big problems in the Middle East in the future. He said it was to be because of "three little letters: O-I-L."

Both Phil and Dave waxed nostalgic about Lanphier's singing program and its center piece, the diminutive but mighty Esther Duncan. If a student was a really proficient singer, he or she would be tapped for the school's renowned a capella group. The not-so-great but still good singers would be relegated to the choir. Ms. Duncan was a stickler for her classes being quiet and disciplined. Here's a story told by Dave about an incident in her classroom he remembers as though it were yesterday.

> If you were talking in class and kept it up, Ms. Duncan would make you go in front of the class and sing a solo, which everyone was scared to do. One day, John Stewart was fooling around and she singles him out to sing a solo. John takes his position in the front and belts out this song Ms. Duncan told him to sing and he's really terrific. She was caught off guard by that fabulous voice and stood there with her mouth wide open. Finally she said to him in her serious manner, "John, you are only the second student in all my years of teaching who has had that wonderful a voice." Unfortunately, John had some personal problems and probably never developed into the singer he could have been.

My sister, Sandy Mitchell ('58), and brother-in-law, Bill Utterback ('55), attended Lanphier in the fifties. Here is a potpourri of some of their remembrances:

- In the fifties, there used to be a gun club at the school and the kids used to bring their guns to school. Wow! That would not happen today. – Sandy
- Leonard Rake was the P.E. teacher before Ed Ransford. Ed used to go to the WMCA to work out (weight lifting) and my friend Don Willet and I worked out with him. –Bill
- For one cent you could get in the gym. Whatever club sponsored these dances bought records with the money. The first record they bought was "Because of You". --Sandy
- You didn't mention "Charlie," the blind man who had a German Shepherd seeing-eye dog. He was allowed to come into the first set of doors and sell his candy bars. I believe they were a nickel. --Sandy
- I loved the Sock Hop we had every year. No shoes allowed --Sandy
- We also remember the strict dress code when we went there: No jeans with metal snaps on them. You had to wear belts. Shirts had to have collars and could not have writing or pictures on them. You had to wear socks with shoes. And no sandals.
- Only one way traffic on stairs; upstairs on the right and down on left. Strictly enforced.

"Russell's" Pizza Drive-In was Lanphier's hang-out in the '50s & '60s. On North 31st Street (North Dirksen Parkway), it was owned by Russell Saputo, a Lanphier grad and later by Angelo and Billie Sue Yannone, who both worked there. Angelo was also a graduate of LHS. It had car hops, seen in this undated picture (around 1960)[Courtesy Sangamon Valley Collection]

Memorial Pool as it looked in my day. This is the big pool (cf. kids pool to the right of the change house) with a diver midflight from the 15-foot board, which we called the "20 ft. board." There was also a 10-foot diving board off-photo to the right. The pool was closed to us in, I think, 1954 due to polio quarantine. c. 1930. It was only a block from Lanphier. [Courtesy of Sangamon Valley Collection]

The hidden, heavy lifters of LHS's building. Two giant boilers that do all the work of heating her...that is, with the help of Head Custodian Randy Blair ('78) and his staff who keeps things greased, clean, and working. These duel boilers replaced the original ones in the 1950s in an expanded boiler room when natural gas became more efficient than the coal-fired ones of the Thirties. [Katie Fitzgerald]

This arial view shows the "Annex" portion of Lanphier High School connecting the Edison Jr. High to the main high school building. It was joined to the schools in 1969, along with the construction of the new "West Gym," in the lower left. [Courtesy of Sangamon Valley Collection]

Chapter 12

The 1960s

The decade of the 1960s represented the dividing line between the relatively calm, innocent, naive days of the forties and fifties and the tumultuous and contentious days of the Seventies and Eighties. My classmates and I were lucky to be in those earlier, carefree days. Whenever I talk with fellow class members, they usually say something like a female classmate and close friend expressed to me over the phone one night: "Ken, we didn't have much to worry about. We didn't drink or take drugs, and we didn't have the pill yet, so there wasn't even much fooling around taking place. It was a wonderful time coming of age. We were lucky in those respects."

The Sixties, especially the latter years of the decade, saw the beginning of an upheaval in our culture brought about principally by the Vietnam War. In Lanphier itself there was an influx of new teachers, mainly Baby Boomers, who brought with them their own set of changes—everything from more casual dress to creative differences in teaching methods and how they related to the older establishment teachers.

One of those new teachers—now perceived old and establishment himself!—explained that he came into the system during a technological revolution in teaching devices. It seems crude by today's standards, but he and his colleagues were using film strips and then graduated to 16 mm projectors. They had to duplicate handouts and tests with those messy mimeograph machines. Lanphier purchased its first copy machine during the 1968-1969 school year and it was closely watched over by the office secretary. VCRs didn't make their appearance for almost 20 more years.

Writing about the years using mimeographs reminds me of what long-time secretary Dorothy Boehner recalled about an episode of a teacher having trouble running off copies:

> Sometimes teachers would use their stencils too many times and caused themselves a lot of problems. Once, this teacher asked me if I would help her clean up the mess—she had ink all over the place. I told her, "Hey, you put more ink than you should have with that old stencil…forget it, you did it, you clean up the mess!" She wasn't very happy but I had better things to do.

The same year I officially became a teenager (13), I started eighth grade at the spanking new Thomas Edison Junior High School, a straight six-block shot from my house on East Converse Avenue and right next to Lanphier. I spent two years there before moving up to the big leagues at Lanphier *Senior* High for my 1959-1960 school year.

I began the year at Lanphier by being accepted into Lanphier's Key Club, an academic organization with a fraternity air to it. It was an honor to be chosen because the inductees had to have at least a B average and good character—whatever that meant. Nobody talked about it in those days, but it smacked of snootiness, and most of the kids probably looked down at it as much as we looked up at it.

I will be finishing off a companion memoir to this book in the near future, writing in detail about my three fantastic years at LHS. So, in this chapter, I will mention just a few of the main events and memories others and I experienced.

One of the contrasting features of those days was that few students had cars and even fewer were allowed to drive them to school. (Remember, there were few "two-car families" and the dad drove the car to work.) Ted Ritter got a 1950 or 1951 Ford that I thought was pretty nifty. I hitched a ride with him on occasion and envied someone who had his own car. When I turned 16, I would occasionally use our family car but more often my sister Sandy would let me use her 1951 four-door Olds Super 88.

My best friend Ronnie Ross and I loved sports cars and brought our copies of *Road & Track* to school with us. Guess what he got for his birthday? A 1958 white Austin Healey Sprite, a tiny two-seater ragtop that was fun to drive and fun to be driven around in. He was one of only a couple of dozen students who had cars at school. (As soon as Ronnie graduated from Bradley as an engineer and landed a job at Sangamo, he drove his new Healey 3000 to my house; he took me for a fast spin around Lincoln Park.)

There was rarely any real trouble in the classrooms in those days. As I mentioned above, we were toward the end of those innocent days when the kids behaved or else got paddled hard enough to make them think twice before causing a commotion again. About the only thing that would get a teacher off-stride was bubblegum chewing or passing notes.

Inappropriate clothing always dogged schools but there wasn't much of that either. In the late '50s and early '60s, boys' pants sometimes came with metal cinch buckles in the back. Since those would scratch desk chair backs, they were banned. Most boys wore Levis with the bottoms rolled up in as small a cuff as possible. I was into clothes at the time and always wore chinos usually with patterned button down shirts. When Key Clubbers went to Kiwanian luncheons downtown with Mr. Petefish, we wore suits and ties. The newer teachers began dressing down after I graduated, first shedding their sports coats, then later even their ties.

Like many adolescent boys, I was terrified of asking girls out. I started out of the dating gate later than most of my public school contemporaries, so I was awkward. Guys like Jay Gobble, Ray Hayes and Randy Powell talked to girls as easily as falling off logs. One of the most gregarious boys, Johnie Knoles, befriended me in junior high and gave me some tips on how to make small talk with girls. He also told me what several of the dirty words and phrases meant; I was totally in the dark on those since I went to a Catholic grade school where they weren't discussed by us boys.

My first social boy-girl interaction occurred when my close friend Jay Gobble invited me to a mixer at the YWCA. We were in eighth grade. He introduced me to some of his grade school classmates and I even danced once or twice. The first date I had was taking Bobbie Kisner to an eighth grade dance in the Edison gym. My dad drove us and that seemed weird to me. Bobbie, a head taller than me, was a sport about it and we both got through those embarrassing early dating episodes. I forced myself to ask girls out and counted a total of 12 or so girls I dated while in high school, with only one that I dated for several months. I relate in detail those trying times in my high school memoir.

I'll mention only one story I tell on myself in the memoir that had to do with a date gone awry. When I was a junior I got enough courage to ask out a sophomore, which was still hard to do. A girl I will call Marsha was a striking natural blonde with a wonderful smile and outgoing personality. I picked her up and took her to Russell's, our Lanphier hangout on 31st Street. We parked and ordered something from the car hop. As we were waiting for our order, Marsha pulled out a cigarette from her purse and asked me, "You don't mind if I smoke, do you, Ken?" I hesitated because it was my sister's car and she would have had a fit if I brought it back with the smell of smoke in it. So I told Marsha she couldn't. If memory serves me, I said it indelicately and I could tell she was quite unhappy. It was all downhill after that. She was so good-looking—she could have been a model— and fun that later, when I had my wits about me, I wished I had let her smoke the whole pack. Heck, I would have bought her a carton just to have a second chance. I ran into her years later in a grocery store and she looked as if she hadn't aged a bit, so she had probably given up smoking. We exchanged small talk and went our separate ways, with me wondering what our children would have looked like.

Two news items I recall during the sixties, shortly after I graduated, were a series of staff changes and a major addition to the school building. In 1965 Miss Norton retired from her teaching at Lanphier and went over to Griffin for several years, teaching them about English and literature. In the 1968-1969 school year Mr. Armitage took over as principal when Mr. Petefish retired to join Miss Norton at Griffin as an assistant principal for a year or so.

Mr. Armitage was born in Lawrence County, IL and graduated from Illinois State University with a B.S. in education. He later received an M.S. at the University of Illinois. He was employed by the Springfield School District for 39 years. In those years, he taught and coached at Hay-Edwards Elementary (starting in 1935); then the same at Feitshans High School (1938-1943); taught science at Springfield High and went into administration— his first principalship at Dodds Elementary, followed at Douglas, Hay-Edwards, and Franklin Junior High, until he successed Mr. Petefish.

The biggest construction improvement in Lanphier's history (costing one million dollars) was ready for the students coming back in 1969. The "Annex" joined Edison to Lanphier to make it the Edison-Lanphier Complex. That name was dropped eventually and nowadays hardly a student or faculty member knows about the junior high that is a vivid coming-of-age memory for me. Then there was the new gymnasium built at the same time. Both those improvements were intended to relieve the overcrowding for several years, but instead gave just a little breathing room for the upcoming flood of students and the accompanying problems it spawned.

The larger, new gymnasium was placed on the southwest corner of the main structure with a long lobby connecting the two gyms. The old gym (called the East Gym or Wrestling Gym or Gardner Gym) has since been used primarily for Lanphier's wrestling program and a spillover for P.E. classes. (That year all three high schools required a daily P.E. program.)

The Annex created one edifice a block long. This windowless, tri-level structure added 20 rooms and a basement cafeteria. Once again, the long-awaited auditorium was scrapped, although the faculty finally got back its lounge which had been used for counselor offices The overcrowding was thus relieved (for just a while), since the capacity of LHS was now 1,600 students, 250 more than what was intended that fall.

Thomas Edison Junior High thus ceased to exist and was converted to additional rooms for Lanphier, which had reverted to a four-year "senior" high school in the 1968-1969 school year. Edison's 21-year run ended because the school board eliminated the junior high system in favor of the middle school model and needed to expand LHS more than it needed another middle school.

At the end of the decade, Lanphier was under new management and about to give the new principal painful insight into what the words rebellion, overcrowding and race relations meant to him and Lanphier High.

Milton Dirst was Lanphier's chemistry and physics teacher for many years. He was my favorite teacher in high school. Demanding, persnickety and caring, he dressed like he respected us and his position. He was also the Key Club advisor during my time. Notice the big teaching slide rule he used. [1961 *Lan-Hi*, p. 116]

Don Post was one of our most popular teachers. He put in 30 years in the district, 16 years of it at Lanphier. He taught Drivers Ed (above) and was baseball coach for 2 years. He remembers everybody's name and attends reunions regularly. They don't come any better. [1960 *Lan-Hi*, p. 11]

An annual city-wide Key Club meeting. Representing Lanphier's Key Club, I was giving a progress report. Seated to my left is Griffin's Key Clubber, Steve Thoma, the Ill-Eastern Iowa District Governor. [1962 LHS Key Club Scrapbook]

Rest in Peace

Glen King was a standout athlete in basketball, football, track and wrestling. He died while a Marine in Vietnam on Sep 10, 1965. I saw his name on the Wall in Washington. D.C. in 1993, Panel 2E Line 80. [*Lan-Hi*, '62]

Folk art mural by one of the Art students, from the 1970s. Students pass by it daily as they walk up and down the Annex staircase. But does anyone really "see" it? [*Lan-Hi's* Katie Fitzgerald]

Chapter 13

The 1970s

The Rebellious '70s

The 1970s was the most chaotic and tumultuous decade in Lanphier's history. It brought about major, permanent changes to the culture and character of Lanphier. Typical of the attitude of the period was the Dedication Page of the 1974 *Lan-Hi:* "Make Your Own Dedication."

Some years back (around the mid-eighties), Mr. Dirst and I had lunch for old times' sake at a downtown drugstore diner. He had taken a job as the administrator of the local Masonic Blue Lodge. (He, Mr. Petefish and a host of Lanphier teachers were Masons.) I was surprised he left teaching; he was a very effective instructor and, as I have said many times to many people, he was the best teacher I have ever had. He responded this way: "Ken, the kids basically ran me off." I couldn't imagine anyone running Milton Dirst off of anything, especially his teaching role. He had as good a controlled classroom management style as any teacher I had in school.

Reading between the lines as I thought through it later, he likely meant the students of the '70s—he left in the spring of 1975 after 23 years—were harder to manage and likely teased him about his relatively rigid manner. But that was a time when the entire country was in rebellion against government and authority, much of it caused by the Vietnam War and Watergate. Out of that sprang a radical change in the culture. Our Golden Anniversary issue of the *Lan-Hi* tried to capture that time period in words and pictures. Here are some of the words:

> ...the Seventies was full of revolts...and wild fads...Lanphier went through many changes in mid and late Seventies...In 1977, rebellion at Lanphier was popular. The year began with a teacher's [sic] strike. Due to an increase in the cutting of classes and vandalism by students, the school district hired the first armed security guard. Key Club protested the integration of females into their organization. The Pep Club revived school spirit in 1977, after almost all traces of it had disappeared in 1975.

When I discussed this decade with Steve Rambach, who started his teaching career at Lanphier in 1967, right before that raucous decade started, he used another example to give me perspective about teachers and teaching then: "Mr. Chiti, for example, was a good teacher and well liked. He used to tell crazy jokes and he could get away with it because the kids respected him. But in the '70s things changed and the kids changed, or else he may have lasted longer too."

Mr. Lober weighed in on that period with uncharacteristic emotion:

> Things really changed starting in the seventies. You talking about Mr. Dirst leaving: I'm surprised we all didn't leave. It did drive a lot of teachers out of the business. I remember when Mr. Brooks would send kids home if they didn't have belts. They used to use the paddle on kids. Talk about change! …And today—when I go to schools, the way the kids dress. And teachers too: you can't tell the teachers from the students. We used to wear suits or at least sports coats.

One bright spot at this time was that the rebellious and rowdy students found a worthy adversary in the new principal, Phil Schmidt, who came to Lanphier in 1974. He had been a student at Lanphier (class of 1952) where he was a four-year member of the football and track teams, and editor of both the *Lan-Hi* and the *Light* (the school newspaper). He graduated from Western Illinois University and then received his M.S. in education from the University of Illinois. He was superintendent of schools in Athens, IL in the late fifties before coming into the Springfield school system.

He was the right man for the right job for the right time. A strict disciplinarian, Mr. Schmidt kept things in line for most of the next 16 years. Not only was he respected by the students, but also joined in with them as the cheerleader-in-chief. He attended all the school functions, and most of the time he wore his black slacks and orange sports coat.

Overflowing with Students

Like other area schools, Lanphier had been running out of room since the 1950s. In a 1964 article in the *Springfield Register* ("Lanphier Most Crowded Of City's High Schools"), Principal Petefish makes the case that his building is bursting at the seams with 1,242 students in a facility made for 750. In addition to the Baby Boomer phenomenon, Petefish points to private schools limiting their expansions and more middle level executives from Bell Telephone and other companies arriving in Springfield. A Citizens School Survey Committee admonished that the capacity could be stretched to 900 by using storage rooms and other such extreme measures. The School Board used these figures to pass a referendum that did combine Thomas Edison with Lanphier in that 1969 Annex/Gym addition, which greatly relieved the overcrowding, but only temporarily.

As school began in late August, 1973, Lanphier was again experiencing large increases in the student body. By school count, 2,356 students caused Principal Armitage to begin to go to double shifts. He admitted that rarely did a Springfield high school have to close programs due to additional enrollments but "we have only so many teaching stations." The 1973 graduating class was about 800 students. Marilyn Gardner, an English teacher and head of the yearbook for several years, commented about the sea of kids in the hall: "The halls were totally packed during the passing periods. You could hardly move. It was something."

When Phil Schmidt took over as principal in the fall of 1974, there was no appreciable decrease in the size of the student body. The huge class sizes continued for several more years. According to Phil Irving (class of '75), the mandatory "split schedule" began the school day with juniors and seniors having first through fifth hour classes from 7:00 AM to 11:55 AM. In the afternoon, freshmen and sophomores attended their classes (sixth through tenth hours) from 12:00 PM to 4:55 PM. He said he and his classmates stayed with that split schedule during all his four years, from 1972 through 1975. Regular scheduled classes returned in the late 1970s when overcrowding subsided.

Chuck Flamini, a future principal who was a social studies teacher at the time (1972-1982), told me that freshmen were actually transported to Lawrence Elementary School during some of this time (mid-1970s) to relieve the pressure. He explained how the overcrowding ended: "It lasted for three or four more years and then just died down. The numbers just shifted and things got back to normal."

The return to manageable levels in the '80s mainly resulted from the demographic shifts Chuck described. Two other factors were partially responsible: (1) the flight to the suburbs, mostly into six Sangamon County suburban schools—Williamsville, Rochester, Riverton, Pleasant Plains, New Berlin and Chatham, and (2) parents (who could afford to) sending their children to parochial schools. That left the Springfield School District essentially as an urban (in fact, inner city) one from then on, with corresponding problems.

Vocational Training

As he was telling me about the split schedule, Phil Irving segued into how vocational education students, such as himself, were bussed to Feitshans daily for their three-hour class. It started at 7:00 a.m., so they could get back to Lanphier for their fourth or fifth hour regular classes and then their sixth hour which began right after lunch.

Phil also pointed out a career advantage high schools had in those days. Lots of students took various vocational courses through Lanphier's VoTech curriculum whereby they basically interned half days at local businesses such as Gietl Brothers (auto body repair), E.L. Pruitt (sheet metal work), Ford (welding) and Phillips Brothers (printing). "Heck," Phil emphasized, "You could walk out of Lanphier's doors on graduation night and walk in one of those shops the following Monday, get a job and earn a nice living, with just a high school education."

What Phil was talking about was a new structured program called Cooperative Work Training (CWT) Instruction that was a logical progression stemming from the old vocational classes that had been around for decades.

Racial Unrest

Although there were still relatively few black students at Lanphier at that time, the racial mix was definitely changing. This was due to the changing neighborhood demographics previously mentioned, plus proportional busing had recently been put into place. All this resulted in approximately 200 black students at Lanphier in

1974 when the incident happened, compared to the approximate 50 blacks when I was in school 12 years before.

Black students started the Afro-American Club in 1973 as a self-identity expression of the larger culture of the times. Its stated purpose was "to help the black students…create a better sense of purpose… [to] strive for a better understanding between the school, black students, and white students." Mr. Curtis Carter was their first advisor.

In spite of this attempt to smooth integration of schools, one of the most divisive times in Lanphier's 77-year history as described below on District #186's website, occurred just a year later in the spring of 1974:

> One of the most difficult events Lanphier has ever faced was the Civil Rights Distribution in the late 60's. Black students were not treated as equals to white students. This caused major problems. Students of all races walked out of school because blacks were not allowed on the cheerleading squad. Students wanted their basic rights. It was probably Lanphier's darkest period in its history.

Phil Irving, a sophomore student at the time, was right in the midst of this challenge. There had never been a black cheerleader at the school and the black students asserted themselves. "It got so bad the principal almost had to close the school," recalled Phil. He remembers the day things reached a tipping point in the spring of his junior year:

> One morning there was a problem when I got to school. Black kids hung out

together in groups as did the white kids. But on that day they wanted to hang out on the front porch [near the main entrance] where we were. There was shouting by both sides.

What he was referring to was the first day after a black candidate for cheerleader had been rejected for the cheerleader squad. Here is the back story of the situation as told by Cindy Luton, a P.E. teacher and a cheerleader selection panel member:

Each year the cheerleader advisor, Sherry Erickson, assembled a panel of teachers to help her grade the tryouts. This black girl was going through some cheers and said she was unable to do the rest of the required ones because she had hurt herself the day before. She was good at what she was able to do, but the panel couldn't know how well she would have done the other cheers. After the evaluation sheets were tallied, all the chosen were white. (There were eight because each would spell one letter of our school name in some cheers.)

The black students thought the whole thing was grossly unfair, especially since there had never ever been a black cheerleader on the team. Cindy continues the story:

The black students had a peaceful demonstration in front of the school, and so Principal Armitage made the decision to expand the cheerleader team to ten girls, and he put the dismissed black girl on the team plus another white girl. Well, the black students were really upset now because of the additional white girl. And the white students were upset because of the reversal in the decision. So the next day both groups showed their unhappiness by picketing classes. They came to school but stood across the street, separately, for some time. But I don't remember things being disrupted much until that last day. There had been tension, but things moved on.

What eventually happened goes down in Lanphier lore. It was one of the most unforgettable days in our history. And every student and staff member at school that day remembers it, albeit in various details. Cindy Luton describes the situation, laughing all the while:

I was actually in the gym trying to teach a P.E. class. Classes were not shut down the previous two days, but let's just say student attendance was sparse. When we heard all the commotion, we ran out and I asked a fellow teacher what just happened.

She said there was a lot of tension that third morning of the standoff, with students segregating themselves into two groups across the street, with the staff and some students in front of the entrance doors. Then, all of a sudden, somebody points toward North Grand and senior Tom Schafer comes racing across the front, streaking *butt-naked,* except for his boots. He then carefully jumps over two hedges on either side of the center walkway and continues running across the entire school grounds, cuts catty-corner across Converse and 11th and into a waiting car at the Sangamo parking lot.

Everybody roared, cheered and laughed. In that one instant, that one wacky act broke the tension. In that instant the whole thing was defused. Most of the students and staff slowly turned and went into the school, and the following day the entire student body returned.

Peace was restored by one student in one premeditated act. As social science teacher Steve Rambach was relating his version of the story to me over coffee, I asked, "What happened to the heroic streaker? Did he get an award?" Here's his response, no longer laughing:

Tom had been selected to be in the National Honor Society. He was an excellent student and a good athlete—[a hurdler, perchance?]— and an all-around good kid, but Mr. Semon, the club's sponsor, was a serious, law and order type and he was not about to allow him to stay on National Honor Society. He had, he said, broken the 'good conduct standard.' We had an NHS committee meeting about it, and a few of us felt he should have been allowed to stay because *he* was the person who broke the tension and defused the situation, even though he did so in an unconventional manner. But our view was in the minority.

The Everybody Club

Steve Rambach noticed during this time that there were lots of clubs at Lanphier but there were also lots of students who weren't in any of them. His solution was organizing a club where anybody could join, didn't have to go to meetings, and could do as much or as little as they wanted. That kind of agenda had hints of the '70s "Do your own thing!" attitude—after all, he created it in 1970 in the middle of the Anything Goes! movement. Even though it sounded hollow at first, it had a deeper reason for being and has become the largest and the longest continuous club at Lanphier.

The underlying story behind Steve's entrance into the club business involved one of his students, Brenda Lael, a junior interested in history who was not allowed into the History Club because of a grade she received as a freshman. The solution? Start a club in which Brenda and everybody else could join so they never had to experience the humiliation she had endured. Steve thought about calling it John Marshall. "It just came to me one day, probably because I had been teaching about his long and distinguished career in my history class at the time Brenda and I talked."

Exclusive to Lanphier, the JMC was formed as "a club with open membership dedicated to uniting the community and spreading the knowledge of former Supreme Court Justice John Marshall." The kids took to it and began expressing themselves in community projects. One of the first was putting on an annual Christmas party for the youngsters at McClernand Elementary School. The next year they made money and, with the financial help from the vocation education classes, purchased the lion statue in front of the school. When a Lanphier student ran a stolen car into it in August of 1989, the club put another right back in its place the following fall. (A teacher told me that very student today in one of Springfield's Finest, thus elevating the concepts of rehabilitation and second chances.) The members also placed two oak trees and two Marshall Elms in front of the gymnasium.

You too can join: all you have to do is say you want in, pick up your numbered membership card and eat an Oreo cookie (Sorry, Steve calls them "John Marshall cookies"). Scott Metzke, the history teacher who took over the club when Steve retired, grew the club, now in its 44th year, from 3,000 to over 5,000, mainly by promoting the historic John Marshall and his namesake club to his and other social science classes. From a snap idea to soothe the wounds of a young student, this club has become an institution at Lanphier and a reflection of what can be achieved by a caring teacher.

Girls' Sports

As if there weren't enough crises at Lanphier and the other schools in the 1970s, controversy reared its head again in the form of inequality in sports. Except for their bowling team, girls at Lanphier and other Springfield schools could not participate in team sports until the fall of 1969, when

Cindy Luton, P.E. teacher, organized Lanphier's first girls' sports team, field hockey. Three years later, the IHSA, the Illinois High School Association, sanctioned Girls Basketball in all state high schools, with the help of the federal Title IX of the Education Amendment of 1972. (That landmark legislation, introduced in the United States Senate by Birch Bayh and signed into law on June 8, 1972, states in part that "No person in the United States, shall be excluded from participation in, be denied the benefits of, or be subjected to discrimination under any education program or activity receiving federal financial assistance.")

Over time, Lanphier's girls' teams expanded further to include basketball, softball, tennis, cross-country, track & field, volleyball, and badminton. For the first dozen years, though, Cindy was strategically lining up how each sport would be introduced: she coached field hockey and basketball; later she switched to coaching softball and basketball teams. Few high school fans ever think how long it took and what a difficult journey it was breaking through the gender barrier. Cindy was there from the beginning, and she can tell you what it was like and that it wasn't always an easy transition. She coached field hockey for six years, basketball for nine years, and softball for ten years. [See Chapter 17 for more on girls' sports.]

Suspended Teacher Controversy

In the spring of 1979, the local daily carried a story ("Lanphier Students Want Suspended Teacher Back," [*Springfield Journal-Register*, March 31, 1979]   about controversial teacher Linda McCoy. The school board took the extraordinary step of suspending the P.E. teacher mid-year for "insubordination to supervisors, did not prepare lesson plans, failed to learn the tornado drill procedures...used racial slurs to black students...criticized students excessively..." The student body was generally split and some vocal students protested on her behalf. A 20-year teacher in the district, the outspoken McCoy fought back with legal counsel; and eventually through court action and arbitration she got the district to drop the charges. After a few more years at Lanphier and other schools, she retired from teaching all together. In the end, it was a battle of wills between a tough principal and a strong-willed teacher.

Marijuana Use

Another issue that came out of the turbulent Seventies was drugs. About 50 Lanphier students picketed the *State Journal-Register* building in reaction to an article it published about life at their school that they felt was unfair. In May of 1979, the paper stated that teachers felt as many as 50 percent of all Lanphier students were smoking marijuana. The students (and even Principal Phil Schmidt) said that usage was greatly exaggerated. Part of the teachers' estimate was based on three back-to-back incidents that occurred the previous week: a dealer caught on school grounds; a bus going out to the vocational school that had to turn around because so many student passengers were openly smoking pot; and a student arrested on school property with a small quantity of weed.

You can see from these various events that the Seventies was a time of profound change at Lanphier and other schools. Yet, Lanphier had a tough principal who was up to the challenge of this time and, as students told me, he was a serious taskmaster and did a good job in keeping the school running as smooth as possible.

The landing at the top of the main staircase at Lanphier holds glimpses of our history: the row of principal pictures excluding the last two) and many of the winning trophies. [*Lan-Hi's* Katie Fitzgerald]

In the middle of the 2nd floor at the top of the stairs is our school emblem presented by the class of 1965. [*Lan-Hi's* Katie Fitzgerald]

This is as close as Lanphier comes to having its own elevator. It was painted on the north Library wall by one enterprising student with way too much time on his hands. Will anyone lay claim to this legendary artwork? [*Lan-Hi's* Katie Fitzgerald]

This portrait of a lion was painted by a Japanese foreign exchange student in 1978. It hangs on the north wall of the main lobby. [*Lan-Hi's* Katie Fitzgerald]

Two Lanphier students make sure their school's flag proudly leads their group on the first Earth Day celebration parade near the Capitol, on April 22, 1970. [Courtesy Ray Bruzan]

FIRST LADY NANCY REAGAN stands next to Angie Smith (C), a Lanphier High School student, after being presented with a "warm fuzzy," hanging around the first lady's neck, by Miss Smith. Lieutenant Gov. George Ryan stands at the left. The students on the periphery participated in the alcohol prevention skit.

Our most famous guest at Lanphier. First Lady Nancy Reagan visited Lanphier and its students at a school-wide assembly on Sep. 18, 1985. [Courtesy *Jacksonville Journal Courier*, Sept. 19, 1984]

Chapter 14

The 1980s

Many Lanphier students, parents and fans think of the 1980s as our sports decade. Lanphier's sports triumphs began with senior Jim Files capturing the State Cross Country title in 1979, setting the stage for a decade of sports success.

Piggybacking on Jim's first-place showing, nothing buoys up school spirit like a championship team, and that's exactly what happened at Lanphier High School in the spring of 1983. Lanphier consistently had great basketball teams, but that year we were gifted with the outstanding athleticism of all its regulars, and especially Ed Horton and Kevin Gamble, both of whom went on to professional basketball careers. Two years later Lanphier won another berth at the State Tournament, coming in a strong second, having been bested in double overtime. It doesn't get much better than that.

The 45-year run of the *Light* was abruptly stopped in 1982 when the school board had a funding crunch and eliminated that budget line item from all the district schools. Mrs. Helen Bellamy Holm, who had been in charge of the paper since she came to Lanphier in 1968, told the principal she would volunteer herself and her student staff to continue publishing it. Mr. Schmidt said emphatically, "No! Because if you do we'll never get the funding back."

It was not until ten years later, in 1992, that the district restored funding for the high school papers. At that point the newspaper staff decided to start fresh with a new name for the then monthly, *The Legacy*. Mrs. Holm stayed on as *The Legacy's* advisor until she retired after the 1998-1999 school year. When classes resumed in the fall, the staff retired the name in honor of long-time advisor Holm and renamed it *The Roar*, which has been its name ever since.

Mrs. Holm told me that in her early years running the newspaper it was a real chore. Here is how she remembers those years:

> We didn't even have a typewriter! We would run up to the typewriting class and ask if we could use one of theirs. Then there was the printing of it. We would send the draft to the printer who put it into two column proofs and returned it to us. Then we had to approve it or make changes and send it back. The whole thing took three weeks, giving a new meaning to the word "*news*paper."
>
> Things changed when computers came in. Lanphier was fortunate to have the district's tech staff housed in our building, which gave us more help than the other schools. It was so easy to publish the paper with the Macintoshes; we could write a 16-page paper without any problem at all.

The Digital Age was confirmed in 1986 when Lanphier's Math Club expanded into the Computer/Math Club under the direction of Mr. Campbell. (It took another generation, in 2001, for Lanphier to get its own digital presence with its own website, as part of the District #186's own digital presence.)

We celebrated our Golden Anniversary in 1987 and published our 50th volume of the *Lan-Hi* with a 16-page spread covering each of the five decades.

During this time a new tradition was started, in 1984, with the beginning of the "King of Hearts" dance. It was a semiformal occasion held in February of each year to honor the young men at Lanphier and has an all-male court. It had a run of close to 30 years but expired a couple of years ago.

A Very Special Guest

First Lady Nancy Reagan visited Lanphier for a short afternoon stop on September 18, 1984, and gave a talk on drug awareness to the student body, reciting the anti-drug phrase she popularized, "Just Say No." This was part of the Reagan Administration's "War on Drugs" to discourage children from engaging in illegal recreational drugs and alcohol by offering various ways of saying no. She said in 1981, when she first became involved in the issue, that "Understanding what drugs can do to your children, understanding peer pressure and understanding why they turn to drugs is…the first step in solving the problem."

That year's *Lan-Hi* observed about the First Lady's visit that "Lanphier was in turmoil for a week prior to her arrival trying to accommodate all of the Secret Servicemen."

Still, it was a real coup that our city and our school landed a visit from the wife of the President of the United States. It is probably true that Bill Cellini, a '52 Lanphier alumnus and head of Illinois' Republican presidential campaign, was responsible for having the First Lady come to Lanphier instead of one of the other Springfield schools. Mrs. Reagan has been the most famous personage to visit Lanphier in its history so far.

The Incredible Mr. Bruzan

Several of the Lanphier teachers and staff I talked to told me I just *had* to include the legendary teacher, Ray Bruzan, in this book. He taught at Lanphier from 1967-2001. Most of us have had one or two teachers who are a cut above the rest. In all my years in school, I can count on one hand the teachers who fit into that category. I had two at Lanphier: Jo Oblinger and Milton Dirst.

I asked Ray what made so many people point to him as one of the greats. He said he had no idea. However, as I spent time with him, it was obvious why he is held in such high esteem. When he began teaching chemistry, Lanphier barely had enough students to fill two sections. Phil Schmidt, the principal, asked him to encourage more students to take chemistry. He had meetings with eligible students and his classes started filling up. When he left teaching in 2001, there were six sections and two additional chemistry teachers. Here's how he described his teaching method:

You and I were taught chemistry the regular way: we were lectured to, given problems, had lab periods a couple times a week, then tests. My approach was more hands-on. Almost daily I had labs and then used the data collected from the experiments for problem-solving. We had maybe only 20 minutes of lectures. That way the students were participants in the process, and they saw value in that.

There was much more to Ray Bruzan than a brilliant teaching method, as transformational as that can be. On April 22, 1970, the environmental movement gave us the first Earth Day. Ray arranged a school-wide assembly kicking it off. Then he bussed some 100 of his students downtown to meet up with other Earth Day students. Ray marched along with them to the Capitol, carrying Lanphier's own Earth Day flag. He had that flag on his classroom wall for years. One day in 1994, the Smithsonian called and asked if it could have the flag and other Lanphier artifacts from that first Earth Day celebration. Lanphier High School now has the honor of having its flag and other items on permanent display at the Smithsonian's National Museum of American History in Washington, D.C. [See a picture of the display in the Appendix.] All of this was thanks to that incredible Mr. Bruzan and his enthusiastic spirit that was infectious to a generation of students.

That, however, was just the start of Ray Bruzan's contributions to Lanphier. Mole Day was designed to commemorate Avogadro's Number (6.022×10^{23}), a basic measuring unit in chemistry. Although he didn't invent national Mole Day, Ray popularized it at Lanphier in a very large way—the "Bruzan Way." There were the Mole Olympics (where students competed to answer chemistry questions with medals for the winners), there were Mole songs, there was the Mole Bowl football game with a Mole Prince and a Mole Princess, there was the annual Mole Guest—one year it was Mayor Ozzie Langfelder ('44) — who wore a Mole suit. These ingenious creations brought more local fame to Ray and his students in the newspapers and on TV. Later came his "Dr. Chemistry and Professor Physics Show," a spoof pitting chemistry students against physics students, which played at First Night Springfield, the local colleges and even University of Illinois-Chicago.

Not surprisingly, Ray Bruzan was honored as the "Educator of the Year" by the Springfield School Board in 1990. He was also Illinois Teacher of the Year Finalist, Illinois Science Teachers Association Honorable Mention, the Rose-Hulman Institute of Technology's Outstanding Teacher, and Illinois' Environmental Teacher of the Year. However, the best tribute is from students themselves, and here is how one summed up this remarkable teacher:

> When I was a student, I admired him most for his energy. He never let his teaching get stale. Our laboratory schedule was always full with the majority of our assignments being experiments of his own creation...The greatest thing Ray did for us as his students was that he challenged us to reach our potential and exceed our expectations of ourselves. [*The State Journal-Register,* May 11, 1990]

Staff Member Wins Lottery

One of the highlights of the eighties at Lanphier was the winning of the Illinois State Lottery by one of Lanphier's own. Assistant Principal and all around good guy Bill Fishburn fulfilled his dream and some would say his premonition. He had a running joke with Principal Phil Schmidt that went something like this: Bill told Phil that on the morning after he won the Lotto, he would toss his building keys onto his driveway for Phil to pick up, which meant of course that he would quit the teaching business. (He only had one year to go at that point anyway.)

They both had a good laugh over this statistical impossibility, but one day shortly after the school year was over, the impossible happened. Bill did indeed toss his keys on his drive but went to school and finished out the last few days of the administrative year. However, he was not there when school started again that fall. He retired on his pension plus the fortuitous $50,000 a year for the next 20 years. After a long retirement of traveling and living in Yuma, AZ, Bill passed away a short time ago.

Large signage with clock and temperature readouts supported by Pepsico for Lanphier and some other District school grounds. [*Lan-Hi's* Katie Fitzgerald]

The lion statue with the historical site designation sign in an arrangement of flowers and smaller statuary. It makes a nice landscaping focus for the front of the school. [*Lan-Hi's* Katie Fitzgerald]

Chapter 15

The 1990s

Chuck Flamini, two years behind me at Lanphier (although I didn't know him) became our fifth principal in October of 1991. Mr. Schmidt moved to the district office and took long-time Lanphier secretary, Dorothy Boehner with him. The history of Lanphier would be incomplete if I didn't tell you something about her since she was in the office for two-thirds of the school's history.

The Office Secretary

Dorothy Boehner was hired as a school secretary at Lanphier in March of 1944, just a year after graduating from Lanphier herself, in the midyear class of 1943. She made her way up to the principal's private secretary and was in that position for most of her almost 50-year run. Like many in her position, Dorothy was definitely in charge. I remember her slightly when I was there in the early sixties, but Cindy Luton has a vivid recollection of her friend:

Dorothy was 'old school' as they say today. She ran a tough ship. For example, when teachers would turn in money from some fundraising project, Dorothy would not accept the cash unless you had counted it correctly, had all the bills facing the same way, and all the invoices and receipts in order. But she helped me enormously in my

P.E. work. I once compiled all the study guides I used into one big binder. In those days all we had were stencil and ditto machines to do the duplication. She came in one Saturday morning and helped run them all off, a big job which she didn't need to do. When she retired she didn't want any big party; instead, she went out with just a few friends.

While we were sitting at Panera East one Sunday morning, Dorothy told me she worked with all the principals from Mr. Stickney through Mr. Schmidt and told us a couple stories about her time at Lanphier:

I always called the principals by "Mr.," even though I knew them well. That was just how we did it in those days. Most of those days are a blur to me but I do recall two stories I can tell you.

One day a lady called and asked me if I was looking out my window and could see all the commotion. I said I saw nothing. Then she said go look out the back door. So when I did, there were all kinds of kids standing outside around the buses. That was when they were having problems over the cheerleader incident.

The other story I remember was when a mother called and wanted to know if her child was in school. I kept telling her she had to call the attendance office. Finally, she said, "Just shut up and listen to me." I let her get it all out and then once again politely but firmly answer, "Miss, you have to call the attendance office."

Royal Campbell, an industrial arts teacher in the '70s and '80s, happened by at Panera's as I was interviewing her, and he told Dorothy that, as a new teacher, he was afraid of her for a long time. She just laughed and asked Steve Rambach, who had driven her to our interview, "You weren't scared of me, were you, Steve?" Steve said, "Dorothy, everybody was until they got to know you."

Mr. Flamini, the new principal, attended Eastern Illinois University where he majored in social studies and competed on the track team. He began his teaching career as an elementary P.E. teacher. He taught at Wilcox, Ridgely, Sand Hill and Southern View. Prior to becoming the fifth principal at Lanphier, he served as social studies teacher and athletic director at LHS (beginning in 1975), president of the Springfield Education Association, and personnel director at SD #186.

Chuck Flamini had an active role to play in the first half of the decade. After four years as principal, he was called by the superintendent to be an assistant superintendent of District #186 and eventually its curriculum coordinator. Chuck was one of those leaders who connect exceptionally well with staff. Everyone who worked under him that I interviewed gave him rave reviews as a principal.

Larry Rowe had been on staff at Lanphier from 1972-1996 and was currently serving as an Assistant Principal in charge of guidance counseling. He took over as principal in the fall of 1996. He was born in 1951, grew up in Ottawa, IL and attended Western Illinois University where he received his teaching degree. He student-taught at Lanphier in 1972 and was hired to teach there the following year. He eventually became the guidance counselor at Lanphier. He was principal for eight years, from 1996-2005.

Lanphier Hall of Fame

To honor all Lanphier graduates who excelled in various fields of endeavor, the Lanphier Hall of Fame was formed in 1991. A couple of years before he retired, Principal Schmidt brought up to his administrators the idea of having a Hall of Fame similar to the one SHS had for years. Larry Rowe, who was an enthusiastic supporter of the idea, asked at a faculty meeting if anybody would be interested in helping to get a Hall of Fame off the ground and running. Eager-beaver teacher Steve Rambach volunteered and, along with a committee headed by Rowe, started researching and eventually came up with criteria for membership and a list of candidates for the first induction ceremony. Steve told me it took him about a year and a half of work developing the entire project.

To be considered, nominees must have attended Lanphier for at least their junior and senior years and graduated at least 20 years before their nomination. They should have achieved national recognition in their field and served as an encouragement to current students.

The first HOF nominations totaled 35; eight were inducted for the startup Hall of Fame team to provide a good base and to include a variety of achievers. Since then, one (and sometimes two) has been selected each year and announced for that honor at a special banquet.

The first inductees were: William Apblett ('39), metallurgist; Donald Baepler ('50), president of U. of

Nevada; William Cellini ('52), first Secretary of Illinois Department of Transportation; Everett Hopson ('40), top attorney for Air Force's Judge Advocate General; William Huddleston ('60), program manager for NASA; Ossie Langfelder ('44), mayor of Springfield; Robin Evan Roberts ('44), major leaguer and Baseball Hall of Famer in 1976; and Claude Sowle ('46), dean of the University of Cincinnati Law School.

Among the other inductees have been: Dr. Sean O'Brien ('80), a member of a team of scientists who won the 1996 Nobel Prize for chemistry; Dean Williams ('59), a still photographer for the motion picture industry; Jack Siebert ('53), who posthumously received the honor for helping develop SONAR equipment at Sangamo Electric used by Navy destroyers; and Alison Novak ('77), owner of Flora Scape and a nationally recognized designer and entrepreneur.

Among the athletes who have been inducted are: Robin Roberts ('44), Baseball Hall of Fame pitcher for the Phillies, and others; "Rocket" Ray Ramsey ('40), professional football player in 10 seasons with the Chicago Cardinals, and other teams and 3 seasons playing pro basketball; Andre Igudala ('02), currently playing professional basketball with the Warriors; Kevin Gamble ('83), professional basketball player with the Boston Celtics, Heat and Kings; Tim Hulett ('78), professional baseball player for 12 seasons with the Chicago White Sox, Baltimore Orioles and St. Louis Cardinals; and Roger Erickson ('74), professional baseball player for five seasons with the Minnesota Twins and New York Yankees.

Always, Innovation Attempts

The district and its schools have always tried out innovative programs and strategies to improve student performance. Several were aimed to help transition students from middle school to high school. Their methods employed a range of sticks and carrots to prod, cajole, motivate and inspire young minds to move forward enthusiastically in academics. They sometimes worked and other times left teachers baffled as their efforts fell on deaf ears. Still, the principals and staff tried and tried, and still try to this day. I will mention several of the attempts— some examples from the '90s and a few more in the 2000s.

The Student Assistance Program is a district-wide plan which has been used as an umbrella for a number of initiatives, from drug prevention to tutoring to the problem du jour. Begun in the early 1990s, one of its main strategies in discussing, for example, drug problems, was taking groups of students and exploring how to prevent students from getting into drug use in the first place; how to help them get off of drugs; and how to mitigate drug use in and around Lanphier.

The Renaissance Program was introduced to the district and to Lanphier in 1994. It was a nation-wide initiative developed to urge students to strive for excellence in the secondary stages of education. To be accepted into the program and accomplish their goals, students had to have excellent attendance and excellent grades. If they won gold (only one absence and a 2.8/3.0 or better) or silver cards (only one absence and a 2.0/3.0 or better), they received special privileges. There was also a recognition assembly where winners were eligible for grab-bag prizes.

A Year of Change

The 1999 yearbook announced that "This [School Year 1998—1999] was a year of change." Those changes included the following: (1) closed campus policy; (2) stricter rules for student conduct; (3) additional Service Learning classes; and (4) a major addition of two new labs and a large community gathering area.

One change not mentioned was an almost inconspicuous changing of the guard in staff during the Nineties. Some of the long-tenured teachers were starting to retire, allowing a steady stream of new blood to enter the ranks. It was hoped that perhaps these young men and women, fresh from university training, would bring new ideas and enthusiasm to the educational process, something sorely needed in these changing times.

Principal Rowe said the school board had no choice but to implement closed campuses at that time. He noted that student excursions throughout the neighborhoods and down to the Avenue were getting out of hand. McDonalds's complained of bad behavior; there was smoking and drug use; loitering in neighbors' yards; and truancy. Closing the campus was the only alternative, especially since we had a brand new area to loiter on our own property, the Commons.

Here's how Mr. Rowe characterized some of the unintended consequences of the closed campus policy: "There was now smoking behind campus trees, which left cigarette butts all over the yard. Kids were patted down and security staff found knives in some cases and so our expulsion rates spiked, not to the liking of the Board. We also had to increase the security force and hired police. A casual observer would not believe that we have 51 entry points or doors into Lanphier."

The Commons

Twenty-nine years after the Annex brought the two schools under one roof, so to speak, another construction project melded them tightly together at the site of the Annex, with an impressive structure called the Commons. It was a two-story and basement extension of the Annex (west toward Eleventh Street) for students to gather and also eat. That 1998 down-sized project (originally 12,000 square feet with three science labs) ended up with two more science class rooms, bathrooms, and a 9,000 square-foot gathering area. Lanphier has graduated between 1,200 and 1,400 students annually since that time, so that added space helped out a lot.

Here's how Larry Rowe remembers the planning, building and furnishing of the Commons when he was principal:

We planned the Commons shortly after I became principal. After our planning an elegant facility, the school board kept reducing the size of the project. It was supposed to be much larger, but first the referendum failed and later funding was cut back. I fought for as much budget money as I could and we got what you see today plus renovation for two connecting physics laboratories.

In that same project we put phones and Internet service in all Lanphier classrooms. We also painted all the lockers in the school and chose colors for the Commons area. We were able to place several large TVs and a VCR system in the Commons area from a donation by Mrs. Phyllis Brooks in memory of her husband. The Brooks' $10,000 bequest—the only one we ever received from a faculty member in Lanphier's history—also included a small endowment for education-related scholarships.

Handling the lunch crowd wasn't easy. We only had 30 minutes for the whole student body, so we had to have two shifts of 600-some students with the volunteer help of teachers reducing their own lunch breaks by half.

This last major renovation project, begun the summer of 1996, was completed in the fall of 1998 and, according to Principal Rowe, "provides us with a contained area that provides restroom facilities, as well as a quiet area to conduct meetings for the school or the district."

Taking full advantage of a new facility, the students quickly decided to build a time capsule. With such items in it as senior class pictures, a video of a pep assembly, a copy of a *Lan-Hi*, a John Marshall membership card, plus several secret items, they sealed it on September 9, 1998 to be opened again 50 years later on the anniversary of the Commons' completion date, September 9, 2048.

The inside of the Commons. There are two rooms; this is the main one where students eat their lunches. Note the TVs along the outside wall. [Photography Class' Cassidy Johnson]

Lanphier High chemistry teacher Ray Bruzan was honored as District 186 Teacher of the Year. He was congratulated by recipients of this award from past years, Melinda LaBarre and Sandra Carlson.

Sponsored by the Horace Mann Companies, the 1990 Springfield Educator of the Year Award went to Lanphier's Ray Bruzan. "With two master's degrees in science, he could have commanded a much higher salary in the private sector, but he finds the rewards of teaching more valuable," an earlier article commented.
[Courtesy of the *State Journal and Register*, September 10, 1990]

School secretary Dorothy Boehner (Rt.), with Carol Statzer.
Dorothy kept everything running smoothly for close to 50 years,
from 1944-1991, with some interruptions for child rearing, etc.
[1976 *Lan-Hi*]

Designation of Lanphier High School property as an "Illinois State Site" took place in March, 2007. At the gathering were Robert C. Lanphier, Sr.'s grandchildren: Lt. to Rt., Robert "Bob" Lanphier III (with his wife Jeanne) and Nancy Lanphier Chapin (with her husband Charles Chapin). [Courtesy of Sangamon Valley Collection]

Chapter 16

The New Century—The 2000s

Steve Rambach was starting his second hour class when another teacher burst in and said, "Turn on your TV, quick!" It was close to 10:00 a.m. on a Tuesday—September 11, 2001. Here's how Steve recalls that historic day in his history class:

> As we watched the day unfold on TV, you could hear a pin drop. No student said a word. No misbehavior. No sleeping in class. Just silence. And it was that way the entire rest of the day. In my class and in every other classroom, all we did was watch the replays and the panic in New York City. I told my classes that "This is like a pebble in a pond. This event will change everything." What the Vietnam War was to the seventies, 9/11 was to become to the nineties and beyond.

Steve was correct in his assessment of 9/11. It changed everything in terms of how we view the world and our place in it. We lost our innocence as we did in WWII. We no longer saw ourselves as an impenetrable fortified nation. We no long trusted others like we did before. We realized we were likely in a very long war against a determined and wild-eyed adversary.

It probably should have wakened students up to the fact that this new world would demand more of them and that they therefore should get busy, get serious, and study harder. But, as you read on, continued efforts with a myriad of programs to build an academically strong student body was met, time and time again, with very mixed results.

Peer Mediation

In 1991, a new program was introduced at Lanphier by Cindy Luton that continued into the 2000s. Calling it Peer Mediation, she designed it to help high school students deal with disputes among themselves in a responsible and peaceful manner. Here is how it came about, in Cindy's own words:

> While some friends and I were vacationing in Wyoming after a stressful school year, we ran into a lady who happened to be a school counselor. That's when I started to complain about how so many kids managed to get into conflicts with one another and with no skills to resolve them. She mentioned a national program she had adopted for similar problems in her Des Moines, Iowa middle school.
>
> The next year Mr. Flamini allowed me and three other teachers to visit this lady at her school and to also observe the program at a local high school there. The program they used was expensive, but a similar program had been started in Illinois. We formed a committee and used information from both programs. Mr. Flamini gave us permission to start it up and he was a huge supporter of it.

Whether students had been fighting physically or verbally, or in other ways unsuccessfully dealing with conflicts, the two students would send in their names to Cindy, and she would designate two peers to the case. The two student peer mediators would meet with the conflicted pair to aid in settling their difficulties. The four students would meet alone in a room and work it out, with Cindy or another teacher outside, just in case. Two of the peer mediators the students requested most were Victor Chukadebe, a Nigerian-born student who had mature listening skills and personality to match and Cara DeRosa, who had the magic touch in tense situations. (Victor went on to play professional basketball in Europe.)

It was wildly successful. In the first year it solved conflicts in over 70 cases. In the following years it averaged around 30-50 cases. Peer Mediation continued for 10 years. After Cindy left teaching in 2001, it continued for a few more years and then lost momentum and finally was stopped.

It baffles me that such a needed and helpful program would ever be allowed to die. Perhaps staff members who read this will consider reinstating the program. It seems to me that it would be needed more now than ever, and its long track record proved its efficacy.

Service Learning

In 1996, Steve Rambach asked Mr. Flamini to be placed in charge of the Service Learning [Community Support] class. Begun three years before by Springfield Southeast's Sandy Wands, this program caught on and grew in popularity around the district. Students in Steve's class signed up for four hours a week to perform services at an organization or school of their choice, their volunteering beginning after that 2:30 class. Steve had his Monday class share their week's experiences—at such places as the Mini O'Beirne Crisis Nursery and the APL Pet Shelter— and also sometimes brought in guest speakers. He arranged for field trips from time to time to show the kids the unsavory parts of Springfield where some unfortunates had to live.

The Service Learning program has transitioned into ACT NOW!, a program in all the area schools. Meeting once a month, the students are encouraged to work together in similar community service projects. Starting with six students, this program had expanded to over 100, necessitating three classes at Lanphier alone. Deb Huffman has enhanced the program so that students may now do service at schools as well as other venues.

Because of his work on Service Learning, Deb Huffman annually hands out the Steve Rambach Service Learning Awards to students who give extraordinary service to the community.

Steve retired in 2003 after teaching at Lanphier for 36 years, but he wasn't yet done stamping his influence on Lanphier. The very next school year he was hired on as Lanphier's College Specialist and Parent Coordinator, a position he developed that encourages students (with support from their parents) to plan ahead and either go to college or have a firm idea for a career path. If you count those 11 years, Steve has had 47 continuous years of service to the students of Lanphier, making him the longest serving teacher in the school's history.

More Academic Programs

The district as well as the staff has come up with program after program in an attempt to reduce academic deficiencies and increase performance, to counter what seemed like an inexorable downward trend in test results. In addition to the programs mentioned in the previous chapter, there was the Bridge project that started around 2000 to give entering students a leg up with a voluntary structured summer program. Then there was reorganizing the home room into Advisories which emphasized personal development strategies.

The next program tried to show students how to view their course content and their place in it with the establishment of areas of study or "Houses"—Arts and Community, Civilization and Change; Culture and Environment; and Freshman House.

The AVID program, the brainchild of an English teacher in an inner city district in California, gradually gained traction in most of the Springfield middle and high schools. The Advancement Via Individual Determination module, which began in earnest in the 2009-2010 school year, teaches students how to increase focus and productivity using specific study strategies. It has been successful and is still in use.

Lanphier Campus a Historical Site

In the middle of the decade, Lanphier's self-image received a badly needed shot in the arm. We accepted some historical fanfare with a photo op and a few speeches.

Lanphier High School became a designated "Illinois State Site" in March 2007 with the help of Lanphier's 1995—2007 yearbook staffs (under the advisorship of Deborah Sidener). In the front of the school there was placed a large black anodized aluminum plaque entitled "Illinois State Historical Society Marker for Reservoir Park and Lanphier High School." With limited space, it tries to tell the back story of its founding. In part it reads:

> ...The school featured the latest in educational facilities and state of the art equipment. Students represented a variety of ethnic groups, families who came to Springfield to work on railroads, in nearby coal mines, and in local industries such as Pillsbury Mills, the Illinois Watch Factory, and Sangamo Electric Company...

Mr. Rowe decided to retire at the end of the academic year 2005-2006. Altogether he had put in 34 years in the teaching profession. The school board placed Jane Chard as Lanphier's seventh principal. She was born and raised in Springfield. After graduating from Springfield High School, she attended Lincoln Land Community College and then received her B.S. in education from Western Illinois University. She later earned her M.A. from Sangamon State University in educational administration. During her career, Mrs. Chard taught remedial reading, math and English. She was the principal at Douglas School before coming to Lanphier.

Morale and Academic Crises

In the 2008 *Lan-Hi* there is an ominous statement toward the front that reads:

"Over the years of Lanphier's existence, the school has gained a reputation that falls short of charming." [Italics added.]

I think what they were referring to was frustration over the achievement gap that has widened over the years between Lanphier and the other area high schools. Notwithstanding all the attempts by the Lanphier staff with the various innovative programs discussed above to increase student proficiency, the students were sinking academically. Testing was at submarginal levels, and that cascaded into morale issues with students and faculty alike. (At the same time, not surprisingly, Lanphier's security detail had to increase commensurately to eight, two police officers and six security guards.)

It was a bad situation that the new Superintendent, Dr. Milton, sought to remedy with a new principal. Some thought it a knee-jerk reaction because Mrs. Chard had been at the helm less than two years and hadn't been given much of a chance to turn things around. Moreover, she had experience as the principal of Douglas School, with student problems more severe than any other school in the district. However, Dr. Milton had the prerogative to hire whomever he wanted, and he wanted Sheila Boozer.

Mrs. Boozer, with experience as an elementary principal, was assigned to Lanphier in 2008. She was born in Columbia, MO and raised in Springfield, IL. She attended public schools and graduated from Ursuline Academy. She attended University of Illinois Springfield where she received her B.A. in psychology and Ed.S. in elementary education, and then an M.A. in educational leadership from Eastern Illinois University. Mrs. Boozer taught at Feitshans, Grant and Durfee Magnet in Decatur. She entered the ranks of school administrator as an assistant principal at Graham, then principal at Fairview. She worked in administration at the school district office at 1900 W. Monroe before coming to Lanphier.

She was immediately confronted with major behavior issues that made their way into the newspapers on a regular basis. She was replaced two years later when the district directive to reduce suspensions and expulsions made matters worse rather than better. Dr. Milton then assigned Artie Doss to the post, another Douglas principal, trying to find the right combination of strength and flexibility in guiding the student body.

Mr. Doss attended Southeast High School where he played basketball, football and track. He worked nine years in the coal mines before going to college, where he earned an A.A. from LLCC, a B.S. at University of Illinois Springfield and two M.S. Degrees (educational leadership at Eastern Illinois University and reading/literacy at Benedictine University). He taught at all three school levels in District# 186 and was assistant principal at Washington Middle School and Douglas Alternative School. Before coming to LHS, he was principal of all three alternative education sites here.

Right when Mr. Doss came to Lanphier, the school district received a federal School Improvement Grant for

$5.2 million (totally $6 million with some other funding), for a three-year period starting with the 2011-2012 school year, with Mr. Doss's arrival. The grant was "to improve education among some of the lowest-achieving schools in the state," announced district spokesman Pete Sherman on June 30, 2011. LHS was among the lowest 5 percent of Illinois schools, according to the State Board of Education.

The money has been used in three main areas: to extend the school day for targeted "enrichment" classes, to enhance professional development, and improve teacher "collaboration" on a daily basis. Part of the funds were also used to hire a consultant to provide training and help track students' progress at Lanphier's new "freshman academy."

After the first year of the transformation grant, students' Prairie State Achievement Exam test scores improved considerably. Before the grant, about 27 percent of students were meeting or exceeding state standards in reading and 24 percent in math; after the first year, they climbed to 39 percent and 31 percent, respectively. The second year's results slid down, so we are all waiting to see what the third year will show.

Since the grant runs dry at the end of 2014, the district is trying to figure out what to do next. It will not have money to continue the extra faculty and the longer school day. So even though the grant provided for new literacy initiatives, extra tutoring, and added Advanced Placement courses (which reputedly increased the rigor in Lanphier's curriculum), the district had to cut budgets for next year to the bone. We will have to see.

A retired teacher told me he was pessimistic about the grant's efficacy: "When they got those first-year PSAT scores [which showed marked improvement] I knew they were not true indicators of remediation because other teachers told me that was one of the best classes in the last 20 or 30 years. You could also tell because the second year's scores went back to pre-grant levels."

Exasperated, he went on to summarize his view about Lanphier's predicament, a view I have heard others express:

It is a shambles, no doubt [referring to being in the bottom 5 percent of state schools]. But the way I see it, it's an economic thing. Springfield [High School] has the west end; Southeast [High School] has the lake; and Lanphier has nothing. We even lost Valley View to Springfield [High School]. The [boundary] lines have always been against us. Still, we have wonderful kids and many good parents. I love Lanphier, loved teaching there, but the cards have always been stacked against us.

Mr. Rowe offered his interpretation of why there had been several long-tenured principals at Lanphier and then three principals in less than five years. He surmised that in an effort to slow down the trend of poorer and poorer academic performance and the corresponding increase in disciplinary actions, the superintendent attempted to bring new blood into the school. The same strategy is sometimes used by corporations: bring in people new to the culture to increase performance and productivity.

He pointed out two factors that made matters worse at Lanphier when the trends began working against it. First, we had an aging facility with smallish classrooms (900 square feet vs. 2,000 square feet in new school buildings). Secondly, the two previous principals had many years of experience at Lanphier and knew the school and its culture intimately, including which programs succeeded and which failed in this north side setting: Mr. Flamini had been on staff for seven years (plus three as a student) before becoming principal, and Mr. Rowe had been on staff for 24 years.

No matter what the theoretical reasons for the plummeting performance over the years at our north-side alma mater, we are a high-poverty school with students from disadvantaged communities. Fact: the majority of our students received free or reduced lunches at Lanphier for many years (Note: "free" meals are now given to all students). Here is how a recent *Illinois Times* article ["Maintaining the momentum: Lanphier High School working to sustain its transformation," May 1-7, 2014, p. 11] describes the present plight of our students:

> Long stereotyped as Springfield's worst high school, Lanphier has worked to transform itself over the past three years…Situated northeast of Springfield's downtown, Lanphier has the highest rate of poverty—64 percent—out of the city's three public high schools. Almost one-fifth of Lanphier's 1,200 students have a disability [mostly special education], and about four percent are homeless, which is double the statewide average of two percent.

Practically every study on this issue tells us academic performance and student behavior are traceable to such factors as family income level. Here's how Randi

Weingarten, president of the American Federation of Teachers, framed this point in a recent *Time* magazine rebuttal to an unflattering article about teachers:

> Two-thirds of what affects student achievement occurs outside the classroom. That's why we need to talk about poverty, segregation and violence in our neighborhoods and schools.

Still, against this difficult and intractable picture, not faced to this degree by the other two high schools, Lanphier teachers and staff continue to embrace their students, ably work with them every day, and do their best to support their academic goals. As a substitute teacher who has spent a considerable amount of time at Lanphier, I can attest to the conscientiousness of its staff. Most, in my opinion, put in heroic efforts on behalf of their charges on a daily basis under difficult circumstances.

At the present time (fall of 2014), it appears Mr. Doss and his staff have things under control at Lanphier. One of the most qualified principals Lanphier has had, Mr. Doss brings a lot to the table: he has a strong background in handling student behavior; he combines a deep concern for the students with a ministerial background (his brother is a minister of one of the largest churches in Springfield); his public relations persona is well received by the parents and the community; and he has an uncommon charisma, especially with the students—something I have seen firsthand as a sub. On top of all that he takes a no-nonsense position on tardiness, dress and rules. Everybody takes Mr. Doss seriously.

Our Aging School Building

So, as we are well into the new century, what's the word on our venerable old building? When I began researching this writing project, I went over to Lanphier and walked down the halls of the main Lanphier building for the first time since I graduated.

Head custodian Randy Blair (class of '78) pointed out the several building additions to me and then showed me the worn asbestos tiles on the original steps and floors. They have served well the nearly 40,000 students who have attended LHS, but 77 years has taken its toll, and they will soon have to be removed with the costly and complex process of an asbestos abatement team.

The terrazzo flooring in the main entrance and central hallway has held up well, together with our iconic circular "crossed stars" insignia in the center of the lobby. It looks as good today as it did 50 years ago when Maggie Shepherd and I sat on it, cutting out decorations for the senior prom and musing about our futures after Lanphier.

There has also been talk in recent years that our aging high school will be replaced with a new school. Randy said if those long-range plans are carried out, it is likely that the newer central building will be retained and new north and south wings will be constructed around it. A local architect who was involved in recent long-range planning discussions with a parents' group explained what he thought a future Lanphier building might look like. His view was that the Edison building will likely be torn down for parking since the present parking lot south of the main structure might be used for the new building. The new gym would be retained as well as the Annex and Commons.

Still another possibility is that the proposed new high school to be built on the west side of Springfield will absorb both Springfield High School students *and* Lanphier's. That would make for interesting bedfellows. With financial woes bedeviling the school district, the new high school is at least a decade away.

A current lawsuit by a student's disabled father wants the school board to put in an elevator so he can observe his son's classes and participate in parent-teacher conferences. Lanphier is the only high school in town that doesn't have wheelchair access to the upper floors—never even a consideration in the 1930s. The board estimates that upgrade would cost $3.5 million dollars at a time when funding is underwater by over $5 million dollars.

Our noble mascot, the Lion, painted on the wall going to the Lober-Nika gym. He also hangs in the Commons. [*Lan-Hi's* Katie Fitzgerald]

Third floor hallway of LHS, facing south from the main staircase. The custodians continue to do an excellent job keeping Lanphier spic and span. Today's students enjoy soft drinks, bottled water (in the picture), and snacks that former students could only have dreamed about.[*Lan-Hi's* Katie Fitzgerald]

Steve Rambach counseling one of his seniors on how to get financial aid for college. He continues his tenure as the longest serving staff member (47 yrs.) in Lanphier history in his present role as College Resource Specialist. [Ken Mitchell]

Steve Rambach in his inimitable way finally got me to "get with it" and join *his* club. He sent me down to Mr. Metzke's history class very recently and I am now an official member. The total count is now 5,663 members. I got to eat a John Marshall cookie too. [Ken Mitchell]

The welcoming road sign into Springfield on East Clearlake Avenue announces the mighty Lions winning the state basketball championship in 1983. [Ken Mitchell]

Chapter 17

Sports

T he Lanphier Lion's sports programs have been a dynamic part of our school since its inception. We will first summarize them on a decade by decade basis and then spend some time highlighting the individual sports.

In 1937, athletic uniforms were different, especially football. The boys' tennis team had a perfect season. Basketball games averaged only 21 points per game. There was a tumbling team in 1938 as well. By 1939 the football and basketball teams won the Central Conference Championships. In fact, the athletic teams had such a great year that the *Lan-Hi* staff summed up 1939 with their first theme—PROGRESS.

The Forties was the time when Lanphier was just beginning to establish a winning tradition in athletics. The varsity football team became the Central Conference champs in 1940. The freshman football team distinguished itself by being undefeated and won the City Tournament three years later in 1943.

The Fifties was a successful time for the basketball and wrestling teams. In 1953, the basketball team became city champs for the first time and continued their city title through 1957—actually co-champs with Cathedral in 1954. During these years, the players captured the regional title and in 1955 they were second in the sectional. Lanphier was one of the first schools to have a wrestling program. In 1956 the wrestling team won third in sectional; in 1959 two of our grapplers went to state. (Bob Nika recalled his days during this period with nostalgia: "Nineteen fifty-five was by far the best year of my life. I was a senior and I met my wife and I played under Arlyn Lober.")

In 1963, a year after I graduated, our basketball team finished third in the State Tournament, thanks in large part to Calvin Petite. (The summer I graduated I played tennis with Cal a few times at Lincoln Park. He was a happy-go-lucky kid who was always laughing.) That was Lanphier's first trip to State. The wrestling team took City three years in a row from 1964 thru 1966. In 1969, the school itself changed when the new gym was added.

By 1974, many girls' athletic teams were already formed, such as field hockey, volleyball, tennis, basketball, and badminton. During 1975, the first girls' golf team was founded, while the first soccer team did not begin until 1977. In 1973, the tradition of excellence began with the first undefeated freshmen wrestling team in Lanphier's history. Basketball also became a symbol of continued excellence when our team won second place in the State Tournament. Jim Files captured the State Cross-Country title as a senior in 1979.

The Eighties proved to be a succession of major sports triumphs. In 1983 the Lions' basketball team finished as the State champs. They returned to Champaign just two years later, in 1985, and took second place. The cross country captured third place in the State in 1982.

Baseball

Ted Boyle took over Lanphier's fledgling baseball team in the spring of 1939. His 1941 team was the first in the city to go to State. He again took them there in 1949.

Don Hudson was a two-time all-city selection and a three-year starter as a pitcher and outfielder in the early Fifties, with the Lions winning the City Series title in '53 and '54. Bruce Boyle, Coach Boyle's son, was all-city and all-conference in baseball in 1953, 1954 and 1955. He won the City Series batting title in 1953 and 1955 and finished second to Feitshans' John Homeier in 1954.

Boyle coached Robin Roberts, Don Erickson, and John Schaive—all future Major Leaguers. His baseball teams had 17 consecutive winning seasons out of his 20 year career. A 1974 Lanphier graduate, Roger Erickson, also went on to pitch in the Majors for five years.

Our baseball teams were again city champs in 1966, 1969 and 1984. We were co-conference champs in 1975 and conference champs in 1978.

Football

Don Anderson came over from Converse school to continue the football program he began when he coached the emerging new Lanphier Lions team at its temporary venue, when they were called the Corsairs. Here is how the local paper described the seasoned coach in its article on his retirement ("Ed Ransford New Lanphier Coach; Don Anderson Quits, Dec. 10, 1957"):

Anderson has enjoyed a successful tenure at the northside school, turning out such football stars as Billy Stone, Ray Ramsay, Ron Little, Walt Ingram, Gene Strode, Fred Yannone, Ron Sexton and Jim DiGirolomo and many others.

The veteran coach began his career as the line coach at St. Viators in 1932 and moved to the head coaching at Cathedral in 1934. Except for a tour of duty in the Navy during World War II in 1944-45, he has been at Lanphier for 21 years.

Our gridiron heydays were mostly the 1940s. We were conference champs in 1940 and Lanphier's 1943 football team remains the school's only unbeaten squad. The only blemish in that 8-0-1 season was a 12-12 tie against Cathedral during which Lanphier's touchdown was called back due to an offside penalty. The Lions had five shutouts in their nine games and only allowed 30 points all season while scoring 252. The captain of the team was Springfield Sports Hall of Famer Billy Stone, who went on to play football at Bradley University and then in the NFL for the Chicago Bears. The left end was Robin Evan Roberts who went on to a Hall of Fame baseball career as a pitcher.

Although our football program over the years has not enjoyed the success of the basketball program, it proved itself a mighty force in its first 15 years. From its first season in 1935 through the end of the forties, the Lions showed the fans 11 winning seasons. Through the Fifties its win-loss record was 107-97-12. Its city series record from 1937 through the Fifties was 9 out of 23 years, with a win-loss record of 28-39-2. It qualified for playoffs six times: 1993, 1994, 1995, 1996, 2001 and 2004.

The 1994 season, with a 9-2 record, was our best season since 1943—and some say our best season ever, due to these four facts. First, we won City for the first time since 1943, and were the first city school to beat Sacred Heart-Griffin since 1975. Second, we won the Central State Eight championship for the first time ever. Third, we were the first public school in Springfield to go to the Illinois High School Association State playoffs. Fourth, it was the first time ever that a Lanphier football team won nine straight games. The next year our team duplicated its win-loss record and beat Sacred Heart-Griffin again. This all happened under head coach John Oakes and assistant coach Jim Cozzolino. Our squads also qualified for the playoffs in 2001 and 2004.

Basketball

Lanphier has had excellent sports programs, some from its very beginning. But some would argue that the two that top the list for consistent performance are basketball and wrestling.

The basketball program's first coach was Hugo Lindquist, who headed the program in the first year at the new school, the 1936-1937 season. For the next 15 years, Rolla Sorrells took charge and did a commendable job, amassing a record 216-161 or 57 per cent.

A young (28-year-old) teacher/coach fresh from four years at Litchfield High School, named Arlyn Lober, arrived for the school year 1952-1953 as the assistant coach. When

Mr. Sorrells gave up the head coaching position, Mr. Lober took over the team and was its coach for the next 21 years, the longest in the school's history. Mr. Sorrells helped as assistant coach for several years. Arlyn told me that "Rolla helped me a great deal. He was like a second father."

Coach Lober's winning record from '53 through '74 was 372-198 or 65 percent. Cindy Luton, a fellow coach for women's sports for several years, pointed out that, "The thing I always respected about Arlyn's coaching was that if he didn't have the best season starting out, he usually ended up with a much better team than he started with. That's the mark of a real coach—consistent improvement." Among Coach Lober's accomplishments were nine city championships, nine regionals, five sectionals, and two appearances at State (third place in 1963 and fourth place in 1971). He was the winningest coach in city history.

At the State Tournament in 1963, the Lions, who came in number three, were one of the first teams to play in the new Assembly Hall in Champaign. The Lions' cheerleading team also distinguished itself by coming in first place. Diane Gobble ('64) told me that her cheerleader teammate, Barb Goulet ('62), made up Springfield's All-City cheer that is still in use today. In it, the girls from all of the schools spell out each school's name in a snappy choreography.

The 1968 boys' basketball team reached the super-sectional but lost to Peoria. Rich Schultz was the standout on that team.

One newspaper article mentioned three quotes from Mr. Lober's retirement roast at the end of the school year (on June 2, 1985) that make me smile every time I read them. Here they are:

> Arlyn was a good coach, and he was always good to his players. Why, one time, one of his kids came in with his report card and he had four F's and a C. Arlyn suggested [to the boy] that he not spend so much time on that one subject. –Ed Alsene, *IL State Journal's* Sports Editor.

> If you were a kid at Lanphier High School and Arlyn said Hi to you in the hallway, that was pretty important. –Bob Nika.

> He's the only man I know whose smile looks like a frown. –Bob Brodbeck, Basketball Official.

Mr. Lober was a quiet man and appeared unapproachable to some of his students. I had him as a math teacher for two years and my tennis coach, so I spent a lot of time with him and knew him well. I can tell you, he was not one to waste words and seemed to be serious most all the time. I always had the feeling that he was multitasking in his head, probably about coaching strategies. In 26 total years of coaching, he had only three losing seasons—that's a heck of a coach. And a legend.

When Mr. Lober gave up coaching, his assistant coach and star basketball player from the '50s, Bob Nika, took over the responsibilities of the team for the next 19 years. He ended up with a record of 257 wins and 245 losses, the forth winningest coach in Springfield history. Coach Nika has the unique distinction of having the only state championship in Lanphier's history, in 1983. That same year his team had a remarkable 30-3 record. His teams made two more trips to the state tournament, coming in second against Peoria Central in 1977 (coached by his old classmate Bruce Boyle) and second again against Mt. Carmel of Chicago in 1985, coming up two points short in a nail-biting double overtime. His teams also won city six times, five regional titles and three sectional titles. For his performance as the head coach, Mr. Nika was named the "1983 Class AA Coach of the Year" by the Illinois High School Coaching Association, the only coach in Lanphier's history to receive that recognition.

Craig Patton was Lanphier's next basketball coach, serving a ten-year period, from 1993 through 2003. His total games stats were 176-106 or 62 percent. Coach Patton's teams won City four times, played in the super sectional and came in second at State in 2002. In 2001, his team had an undefeated record of 14-0 in the Central State 8 Conference.

Lanphier has had four coaches since Patton, and they have shown the same kind of consistency its basketball team has always had.

For those kinds of team records, we were blessed not only with superior coaches but some remarkable players. Among them are our All-City Players: Ivan Jackson ('57); Cal Pettit ('63 & '64); Richard Schultz ('68); Jim Zimmerman ('69); Jim Kopatz ('71 & '72); Kevin Gamble ('83); Ed Horton ('85 & '86); Jeff Walker ('95 & 96); Victor

Chukwudebe ('96); Richard McBride ('01, '02 & '03); and Andre Iguodala ('02).

The highest scorers in Lanphier's history were Ed Horton in 1986, with 852 (25.8 points per game) and Andre Iguodala in 2003, with 800 (23.5 points per game). Gamble, Horton, and Iguodala have played in the NBA and all three have come back to Lanphier to put on basketball summer camps, a kindness not lost on the Springfield community.

Arlyn reminded me that some of the individual records were skewed "when you remember that during those years when Lanphier was a senior high school, athletes had to compete for records with only three years of playing. For example, and there are plenty more, Cal Pettit was a fine player who could have broken scoring records if he had four years to do it in. Even with three years, he was voted by one Florida paper as 'All-American'."

Although Gamble, Iguodala and other players were well known as superstars, I would like to point out four players—there are others as well, especially from the early years— whom history has shortchanged to some degree, or are unknown to the younger Lanphier students and alumni.

Don Erickson, the first of several Major League Baseball family members from the Springfield area, was all-city in both 1949 and 1950 basketball seasons and led the city in scoring. He once scored 52 points in a YMCA League basketball game.

Ivan Jackson, one of the 2014 Springfield Sports Hall of Fame honorees [See the Appendix for a complete list of

Lanphier's inductees.], is lesser known, yet one of the powerhouse basketball players in Lanphier's annals who deserves remembering. When he graduated from LHS in 1957, his 1,374 career points were the most in school basketball history, and he's still among the top 10. He was a two-time all-city pick (1956 and 1957) and he led the city in scoring as a senior in 1957. With an average of 21 points per game, he became the first Lanphier player ever to average 20 points a game. In effect, "Jackson helped elevate Lanphier basketball to heights previously unseen," one example being that he was also "the leading scorer for all the schools in our first sectional title in 1956." [*IL State Journal-Register,* Mar 22, 2014]

Richard McBride has the distinction of being Lanphier's all-time career scoring leader with 2,032 points. He led Lanphier in scoring in years 2000, 2001 and 2003. He was the second player at our school to pass the 2,000 point mark.

Ed Horton, currently on Lanphier's staff, accomplished much in his time here:

- The only Springfield player in history to earn "Mr. Basketball" in Illinois after leading the Lions to a second-place finish in the 1985 state tournament.
- The only Springfield athlete ever to earn All-Big Ten honors in basketball
- The highest scorer in school history in 1986 (852, 25.8 points per game)

- The No. 2 rebounder in school history (877 rebounds, 6.6 per game)
- Drafted by the Washington Bullets on the second round of the 1989 draft with the 39th pick and played a season in the NBA
- Played basketball in the Continental Basketball Association and all over the world in Italy, France, Israel, Chile and Puerto Rico

With our excellent coaches, players and the occasional superstars, Lanphier High School has gotten to State many times—the true mark of a great basketball program. We participated in ten Sweet Sixteen appearances and had six Final Four appearances (3 with Nika, 2 with Lober, and 1 with Patton). We also have the highest percentage of City wins, and in 2002, we had the highest victory total in the state—32/2.

Wrestling

Ed Ransford is the person responsible in large part for bringing wrestling programs into the Springfield high schools. After his Army Air Corps days as a World War II bomber co-pilot, he attended the University of Illinois where he earned a degree in Physical Education and began his teaching career at Ridgely and Bunn grade schools. After two years there, he was transferred to Lanphier in 1953. At Lanphier, he was the jack of all trades: athletic director and coach for basketball, football, golf, and track and field.

In 1955, Ransford introduced wrestling to Lanphier, the first school in the city to have the program and later encouraged his friend, John McCoy at Feitshans, to start a program there. He coached Lanphier's wrestling program for the next eight years. I had Mr. Ransford for P.E. classes during my three years at Lanphier and was impressed with the seriousness with which he conducted the classes and himself. I remember hearing that he had been a Golden Gloves boxer, but I had not known about his air corps days.

I was also impressed that he would regularly do calisthenics along with us, as well as run the track when we did. After school, I would see him again running around the practice track. He was in great shape and wrestled with his grapplers as I mentioned before. Years later I saw him visiting his wife at my mom's nursing home and I commented on his physical regimen back then. He laughed with that full-out smile of his and responded, "People used to tease me staying in shape like running the track every day, but now days they would say I was using a wellness lifestyle."

Ransford's coaching paid off right away, with three of his grapplers representing Lanphier in both the sectionals (coming in fourth) and in the state championships in Champaign in the winter of 1955. Sophomore Paul Gebhart placed in the 95-pound category, Frank Nudo placed in the 138-pound category, and Floyd Bee placed in the 103-pound category. As the Springfield newspaper put it, "[It was] the first time in history that the city of Springfield had representatives in the state high school wrestling finals... Coach Ransford and his three champs, Gebhart, Bee and Nudo." [*Illinois State Register*, Feb. 25, 1955]

One of Coach Ransford's biggest accomplishments was mentoring senior Julian "Babe" Gabriel who came in third at 154 pounds at state in 1964, the first city state-meet placer. That was no easy task, getting "Babe" to do anything. (He threw a snow ball at me when he was 12 and then beat the tar out of me when I confronted him.) His brother, Mike, who was a classmate and friend of mine, was also a formidable wrestler two years before, but not as strong for his class as his little brother. "Babe" had a ferocious temper and attitude to back it up, but somehow Coach Ransford marshaled him along both in football and wrestling, bringing out the best in him with some sort of magic. (Babe didn't fare as well in life, ending up in prison and recently dying there.)

When Mr. Ransford gave up wrestling after the 1963-1964 season, Lloyd Atterberry filled in the next year. Then an outstanding athlete in his own right named Jim Gardner took over in 1965 and really put Lanphier on the map in wrestling. "Gardner" and "wrestling" are two words used together whenever Lanphier wrestling is mentioned. He was such a success over the years that the old gym is now the "Gardner Gymnasium" in his honor.

Gardner was an all-around star athlete at Feitshans, then the same at Eastern Illinois University, where he concentrated on wrestling. He was team captain his junior and senior years and a two-time NAIA All-American. As a junior he placed third at 167 pounds in the NAIA national meet and set an NAIA quick-fall record, 20 seconds. As a senior, he was Eastern Illinois' first NAIA champion, winning the 177-pound title. The Springfield Sports Hall of Fame website continues his bio sketch:

He had a 50-18 career record with 25 pins and holds EIU records for most consecutive pins (6), quickest pin (20 seconds), most pins in a season (10) and most career pins. He served as a graduate assistant in wrestling at EIU in 1962-63, then spent 1963-65 as an assistant coach at West Leyden High School in Northlake before taking the head coaching position at Lanphier in 1965 until his retirement from teaching in 1994, when he became an assistant...he's a member of the Eastern Illinois Hall of Fame [1984] and the Illinois Wrestling Coaches and Officials Hall of Fame [1986].

Coach Gardner has a few more distinctions: He was the 1979 *Illinois State Journal-Register* Coach of the Year; he was the Grand Marshal of the IHSA Wrestling State Finals in 1993; he received the Lifetime Service Award from the National Wrestling Coaches Hall of Fame in 2003; and he was the recipient of the Lifetime Achievement Award of the Illinois Wrestling Coaches of America in 2003.

His accomplishments at Lanphier are legendary. Once again, quoting from the Springfield Sports Hall of Fame website:

Gardner-coached wrestling teams won five conference championships, six regional titles and one sectional crown, and he had 74 state qualifiers, 27 sectional champions, 25 state placers and one [class AA] state champion [his son, Andrew at 105 pound in 1988]. His teams also won 431 dual meets, and during the offseason he spent 15 years coaching the Lanphier-Southeast Wrestling Club with seven placers and two state champions.

Gardner's son, Andrew or "Drew," was probably the best wrestler to come out of Lanphier High. In addition to winning the class AA State Championship, Drew did the following, as mentioned on a plaque in the wrestling trophy case in the main lobby:

> He rewrote the Lanphier wrestling book: Most consecutive wins 62; Most career tournament wins 25; most career wins 151; most career pins 85; Best in weight, 98, 105 and 112; Best Record for 4 years Varsity, 151-8; and Best record for 1 year Varsity, 40-1.

Unfortunately, there were two tragedies that affected his team and himself during Coach Gardner's career. One of the most promising freshmen grapplers to ever come through his program died in a motorcycle accident in 1975. Dale Monroe set the following J-V records during his one-year career at Lanphier: Most Consecutive Wins (season and school), 17; Most Wins (season and school), 24; Most Consecutive Pins (season), 6; Most Pins (season and school), 18; his record was 22-2 (losing in J-V competition to a sophomore and a senior); Freshman-Sophomore Conference Champion; Lincoln Invitational Champion. His fellow wrestlers thought so much of him that they voted him Most Valuable Wrestler. Coach Gardner said Dale was his finest freshman wrestler.

They say the worst tragedy that can befall a parent is losing one's own child. Jim and Marilyn Gardner had to endure that unspeakable experience when their son Jeff was also killed in a vehicular accident in town. Another extraordinary wrestler from the Gardner family, Jeff was also destined for greatness. Coach Lober told me that Jeff would likely have placed first in state had his life not been cut short. His record was stellar. [See his stats and those of his siblings in the Appendix: "Those Awesome Gardner Boys."] Here is how long-time local sports writer Gene Seymour described Jeff's abilities in a tribute to him shortly after the accident:

> Jeff was, to date [1983], the most successful wrestler produced from an outstanding wrestling family. Gardner placed sixth last year in the Class AA State Wrestling Tournament at 112 pounds. In two varsity seasons, Gardner had a record of 68-7... With two high school City Wrestling Tournament titles, Gardner was a strong favorite to be the second four-time city champ by his senior season. That his wrestling success would have carried into college was a foregone conclusion.

To honor Jeff's memory, the Jeff Gardner Memorial JV Tournament was established.

An article in the *State Journal-Register* announcing Gardner's retirement ("Wrestling with Retirement," Dec. 11, 2008) summed up Coach Gardner's motivation when his wife, Marilyn (also a Lanphier teacher and wrestling scorer and photographer) mused, "Kids are in wrestling because they want to be. They're not always in English because they want to be. They have to be there or they won't graduate." The Coach added, "We've still got kids who do what we ask them to do. They haven't changed that much."

Track & Field and Cross Country

Lee Halberg changed the face of Lanphier's track and cross country history since taking over in 1972. He had great success himself as an athlete at Springfield High School ('65) and won the city pole vault champion as a junior and later competed in the intermediate hurdles at the University of Missouri. He coached successful track and cross country teams at Plainfield High School in the four years before coming to Lanphier.

Halberg coached here from 1972-1989. And through those 16 years, his teams dominated both sports on the local scene. His 1982 cross country team placed third in the state, the highest ever by a city team and one of the best in the more than 50-year history of the meet by a downstate team. Five times between1978-89 his teams placed among the top 10 teams in the state meet.

His boys' cross country teams won 14 straight City Meet titles between 1975-88, and the boys track teams began a run of City Meet titles in 1977. In 1979 one of Halberg's runners, Jim Files, won the Class AA state cross country title. Here's how Files' accomplishment was described in "50 Years of Illinois High School Cross Country," a booklet compiled by Springfield sports writer Jim Ruppert:

The Class AA individual field is billed the deepest in the 34-year history of the meet. But it is a relative unknown, Jim Files of Springfield Lanphier, who emerges as the state champion in 14:18.3. Files becomes the first state champion in the one-class or Class

AA meets from south of Interstate 80 since Craig Virgin in 1972. Ralph Caron of Chicago Marist, who admits afterward that he didn't know who Files was, finished second in 14:19.

For leading those remarkable teams, Lee Halberg is a seven-time winner of the South Central Illinois Track and Cross Country Coaches Association's Coach of the Year award in cross country and track and was inducted into its Hall of Fame in 2001. He is also a 1998 inductee into the Springfield Sports Hall of Fame.

Just as Bob Nika went on to make a name for himself after Arlyn Lober retired from basketball, Mike Garcia carried forward in the steps of Lee Halberg when he came to Lanphier in 1990. Garcia is still teaching and coaching, after 24 years (going on 25)—the longest tenure of all of the LHS track and field/cross country coaches. He has twice qualified teams at Lanphier for the State Meet. He has coached athletes to State medals in cross country five times. In track and field, Garcia's teams earned the third place trophy at State in 2007, 2008, and 2009. He has coached five State champions and over 40 State medalists.

Most if not all of the school's track and field records have been broken during his tenure. Garcia's teams have won many city and conference Titles. In addition, many of his athletes have gone on to enjoy successful careers in college. Lee Halberg sums up Garcia's career in one sentence: "Mike is held in the highest regard by high school and college coaches in Illinois and the Midwest." Like Halberg, Mike Garcia has been honored by his coaching peers for inclusion in the Illinois Track and Cross Country Coaches Association Hall of Fame in 2009.

Girls' Sports

As I mentioned in Chapter 13, girls sports didn't begin until the school year 1969-1970 when Cindy Luton introduced field hockey. Volleyball was off and running by 1973 with a 6-6 season. Its 1986 record was 22-4 and the team won the Mid-State Ten Tournament. Here is a summary of some of the major highlights and outstanding players in girls' sports.

Girls' basketball, which began in 1972, developed well and has been successful over the years. As a matter of fact, it won its first City Tournament the very next year, 1973. It had a 25-6 season in 1991, together with first places in city, regional and section tournaments. It again won city the following year. It has won regional six times (in 1984, 1986, 1990, 1991, 2005 and 2006). Among long-time coach Mark Scheffler's all-city players were Valencia Foster, Donetta Coleman, and Andrea Downey.

Girls' softball won Regionals in 1980, 1981, 1982 and 2002.

Girls' Volleyball has been around since 1973, and its team came in second in the city tournament the same year. Coach Mark Sheffler has had the most success with the team. He coached them from 1981 through the 1988 season, earning a 136-84 record. Coach Scheffler's all-city selections were Valencia Foster, Sonya Kunz, Mindy Sanders, and Patty Brunner.

Girls' track and field won district in 1976 and sectional in 1999. Sherri Weiskopf holds the school record for the 800 meter dash. In 1992 Susie Newell, a senior, won the Class AA State high jump title (5'9") and became the Lady Lions' first ever female state champion. She finished first in every outdoor meet in 1992. Coach Scheffler's all-city selections were Lisa Petro and Susie Newell.

Girls' cross country began at Lanphier in 1975-1976. In 1981, Lanphier's Cathy Rodkey was the first female from the city to qualify for the Illinois Cross Country State Meet. She finished 84th. That same year the team won district and conference championships. The girls' cross country was first in city in 1988 and was number four in conference and regional tournaments.

Special recognition has to be given to Jennifer Smith ('91). Here is what the Springfield Sports Hall of Fame says about her on its website. She was inducted into it in 2012.

Jennifer was a standout in volleyball, basketball and softball. As a senior in 1990-91, she led the girls' basketball team to a Supersectional berth—Lanphier was the first Class AA city school to qualify for the Supersectional--and a 25-6 record. She was all-city in softball four times, all-city in basketball three times and all-city in volleyball twice. She was both the basketball and softball Player of the Year in 1989-90 and 1990-91, and as a senior she was named first-team all-state in basketball by the *Champaign News Gazette*. She was named State Journal-Register Female Athlete of the Year in 1991.

She played softball on the Illinois Central College team that finished seventh in the nation as a freshman, but she was diagnosed with rheumatoid arthritis and had to give up competitive collegiate athletics. Since her sophomore year in college she has undergone 24 surgeries -- including five joint replacements -- and is blind in her left eye. Nevertheless, she still bowls four nights a week at a very high level and is a regular on the golf course.

I was unable to find very much information about some aspects of Lanphier sports on the Illinois High School Association's website; for example, the history and records for Lanphier boys' soccer, golf, and tennis. I had even more trouble getting information on those same sports for the girls. Same goes for our last few seasons. Hopefully, some enterprising sports enthusiast will find time and motivation to bring these sports up to date. If he or she does appear, I will be happy to put the information in future printings of this book. Wouldn't it great if someone would write a comprehensive book on Lanphier's sports program (along with pictures), giving the recognition it and its athletes deserve?

The Lanphier fight song likely originated toward the end of when the students used Converse High as the predecessor to their new school. This copy was dated 1969. [Courtesy Sangamon Valley Collection]

Conclusion

There are four threads that run through our history that I would like to make a few observations about.

First, things have a way of running their course, be it staff, programs or activities. I mentioned a number of aggressive initiatives that were started in the late '80s and '90s at Lanphier. Key Club is another case in point. I spend a lot of time talking about it in the book because it was a top tier organization at Lanphier for many years and a major influence on me during my formative years. Yet, it petered out in the early '90s because times change and people change. It was no longer needed, and other clubs took over the service activities it once provided.

Second, the right person seems to emerge to solve particular problems at just about the right time. Mr. Schmidt came along when students began changing the culture of the school. And just at that point a strong disciplinarian was on the scene. In the same way, Mr. Petefish and Mr. Dirst were around when Key Club was a major influence, and they did a great job marshaling us along the leadership path.

Third, history is flawed. By this I mean that as hard as I have tried to be a faithful recorder of the true events that shaped Lanphier, I probably left some important things out. Or I misinterpreted them or simply got them wrong. A chief means I used to avoid such historical inaccuracies was to interview a number of people in each decade, especially some of the principals themselves. Of course, they responded with their own perspectives, telling their own truths about their times. I also tried to tell the truth of the school, "warts and all." Still, in the end, I think that we have a pretty good representation of what Lanphier's history is all about. It sure is a lot more than was available in one place when I started.

Fourth, my hope is that the Lanphier culture will circle back and in some ways resemble the golden age I was a part of in the early sixties. They say history repeats itself, and I would be pleased if it did so by way of a return to a less complicated structure and simpler response to problems. I have an intuitive feeling that Lanphier would profit immensely by a rebirth of Key Club with an enthusiastic Kiwanian Club to support it and a compatible teacher(s) to advise it.

Many of the alumni I interviewed gushed over their experiences of attending Lanphier. I can say without hesitation that I also enjoyed to the fullest my days in the sun at this wonderful school. I loved my high school days and think of them often, especially as I stroll its halls substitute teaching. Lanphier was my sanctuary, my new family abode, my adolescent laboratory. I hope you feel the same way about your days there or wherever you spent your high school years.

Works Cited

Antonacci, Hugo, *The Life and Times of Hugo Antonacci*, Springfield, IL, self-published, December 1998.

Cavanagh, Robert, "Robert Lanphier Lights up Springfield," *Illinois Times*, June 10, 2004.

Davis, Cullom and Wrigley, Kathryn, *Memorial Days: A History of Community Partnerships 1897—2007*, Springfield, IL, Memorial Health System, 2007.

Hohne, Howard, "A Boy's Park," Springfield, IL, self-published article, 2014.

"History, Lanphier High School," <www.sps186.org/schools/lanphier/?p=277&b=51&cat=> September 13, 2014.

Kohlrus, John A., *Family*, Springfield, IL, self-published, 2007.

Krohe, Jr., James, *Midnight at Noon: A History of Coal Mining in Sangamon County*, Sangamon County Historical Society, Springfield, IL, 1975.

LaFata, Paul, M.D., *My Story: Determination, Hard Work and Faith*, Springfield, IL, self-published, 1997.

Langfelder, Ossie, *My Incredible Journey*, Springfield, IL, self-published, 2010.

Lanphier, Alfred Young, CDR. USN/RET, *Autobiography*, New York, NY, self-published, 1970

Lanphier, Robert C., *40 Years of Sangamo,* Chicago, IL, privately-published, 1936.

Mitchell, Kenneth C., *Converse Kids: A Memoir on Growing Up,* Springfield, IL, Seagull Press, 2009.

Mitchell, Kenneth C., *Rabbit Row: The Life and Times of J.P. Mitchell,* Springfield, IL, KM&A
Press, 2004.

Mitchell, Kenneth C., *Sister Raphael: The Life of Jennie Roscetti Mitchell,* Springfield, IL,
Seagull Press, 2006.

Russo, Edward J., Mann, Curtis R., Garvert, Melinda, *Springfield: A Reflection in Photography,*
Charleston, SC, Arcadia Publishing, 2002.

"Samuel A. Sgro Memoir," SG67. Interview and Memoir, 1 tape, 60 min., 14 pp., by Jim Krohe, 1972, University of Illinois at Springfield, Norris L. Brookes Library, Archives/Special Collections.

Shadid, Phil (and Nanninga, Dave) "Springfield Converse High School 'Corsairs,'"
<www.illinoishsglorydays.com/id583.html> 2014.

Springfield Boys' High School Basketball Summaries: 1911—2005, Tom Fitch, Springfield, IL, 2005. CD.

"Springfield North Revisited…a Celebration," a 15-page supplement, *Springfield Journal-Register*, May 5, 1958. It has a list of two dozen citations for more local North-End history.

The Lanphier Light, Vol. 1, Number 4, April 1, 1937, Springfield, IL.

Historical Resources

A. Here are two important local historical go-to places in central Illinois where you can access books, stories, documents and archives.

Sangamon Valley Collection

The Sangamon Valley Collection (SVC) is on the third floor of Springfield's Lincoln Library. It was established in 1970 through the support and encouragement of the Sangamon County Historical Society. It serves as a regional local history and genealogy collection for Springfield, Sangamon County, and all eleven of its bordering counties— approximately a 50-mile radius. It collects, preserves, and provides information through a number of formats, including photographs, books, newspapers, maps, directories, yearbooks and surveys. Visit the SVC in the Lincoln Library at 326 S. 7th Street, Springfield, IL 62702. Call 217-753-4900, ext. 234. The website is: www.lincolnlibrary.info/research/sangamonvalley.html. Curtis Mann, Manager, Curtis.Mann@Lincolnlibrary.info.

Sangamon County Historical Society

The Sangamon County Historical Society is devoted to preserving and promoting the history of central Illinois. Since 1961, society members have fulfilled that mission by organizing monthly educational programs, tours of historical buildings and museums, developing special projects, and publishing a monthly newsletter, as well as various books and booklets on area subjects. The Society regularly collaborates with area historical organizations to develop programs for the community and has participated in major restoration projects at area sites such as the Old State Capitol, Executive Mansion and the Elijah Iles House in Springfield. It also is a proud supporter of the Sangamon Valley Collection which collects research materials related to Springfield, Sangamon County and its adjacent counties. See its website: www.sangamonhistory.org.

B. If you are interested in more school history, the *Lan-Hi* staffs wrote two historical documentaries that I have quoted from in this book:

- A wonderful five-page retrospective ("Our Heritage") in the front of its 1954 annual that covers little known information on the early curricula, discipline, examinations, and regulations; and
- A colorful and expansive 16-page retrospective spread, with lots of period pictures, in the semi-centennial 1987 annual.

C. There are also several websites you can reference which have, to varying degrees, some Lanphier history, pictures, comments, etc.

- www.sps186.org/schools/lanphier/info/history This is the official School District 186 website

- www.LanHiOnline.com by Lanphier archivist and historian Randy Miller ('71). Randy has populated this friendly site with yearbook pages, pictures, memorials, free classified ads, and Lanphier Light pages, over many years.

Appendix

Curtis Mann, Manager of the Sangamon Valley Collection (SVC) on the third floor of the Springfield Lincoln Library, is giving me a few pointers on researching. Curtis and his team provide valuable services to local historians and students.

Lanphier High School Milestones

1866	Reservoir Park built
1870	Illinois Watch Company founded by John Bunn et al.
1897 the	Jacob Bunn, Jr. takes over as president of Illinois Watch Company
1899	Sangamo Electric Company organized with Jacob Bunn, Jr. and Robert C. Lanphier as principle managers
1925	Reservoir Baseball Stadium opens
1926	Jacob Bunn, Jr. dies
1928	Illinois Watch Company sold to Hamilton Watch Company
1930	Pillsbury Mills begins operation near Lanphier
1931	Ninth grade is added to Converse School
1933	Reservoir at the Park is torn down by WPA Workers
1934	All four years of high school are added to "Converse High School" Mr. George Stickney is Principal of CHS
1936	Construction begins on Lanphier High School

1937	Classes commence at LHS and first class graduates in May
1939	Robert C. Lanphier dies
1940	North wing to LHS completed
1948	Band room added to LHS
1949	Memorial Stadium opens
1957	Charles W. Petefish begins as Lanphier's second Principal; Boiler room expanded as well as Voc Ed rooms
1968	John W. Armitage begins as Lanphier's third principal
1969	An Annex connects Thomas Edison building to LHS; west gymnasium opens; Lanphier forms girls' sports teams
1974	Phil Schmidt begins as Lanphier's forth principal
1978	Sangamo Electric Company's Springfield Factory closes
1979	Lanphier's Jim Files wins state cross country title
1983	Lanphier Basketball team captures State Division II title
1984	First Lady, Nancy Reagan, visits Lanphier
1985	Ed Horton receives the Illinois "Mr.

Basketball" award

1988	Andrew Gardner wins the Class AA state wrestling championship (105#)
1991	Chuck Flamini begins as Lanphier's fifth principal
down	Pillsbury Mills Springfield operation closed
	Lanphier Hall of Fame begun
1996	Larry Rowe begins as Lanphier's sixth principal
1998	Commons area added onto the Annex
2006	Jan Chard begins as Lanphier's seventh principal
2007	Lanphier's location designated "An Illinois [Historical] State Site"
2008	Sheila Boozer begins as Lanphier's eighth principal
2011	Artie Doss begins as Lanphier's ninth principal Lanphier receives $5.2M Federal School Improvement Grant

Principals

It is a compliment to the School Board and Lanphier's administration that we have had only nine principals in the high school's 77-year history. Here is a bio sketch on each of them.

#1 **George E. Stickney** (CHS: 9/1934—1/27/37: 2 1/3 years; LHS: 1/25/1937—1/1957: 20 years) was Lanphier's first principal who shepherded the new high school through its formative years. He was also its longest serving principal. He began as a teacher, later a principal and then school superintendent in Adams County, IL. He came to Springfield in 1927 and was principal of Lawrence Elementary School until he became Lanphier's head administrator. After his tenure at Lanphier he accepted the post of Director of Secondary Education at District #186, where he organized the junior high school program. He then held the position of Assistant Superintendent of Schools for the last three years of his career. He retired in 1961 and left Springfield. He passed away five years later.

On the 20th anniversary of Lanphier's founding, Principal Stickney was honored in the gymnasium with a tribute program where he was presented with a color oil portrait of himself, painted by Mrs. Grace Woodruff, to be hung in the school building. Today you can see him still looking down on those students who are coming up and down the main staircase, along with the other principals, just above the awards and trophy cases that line the landing.

#2 Charles W. Petefish (1/1957—6/1968: 9 1/2 years) was born on a farm near Carpenter Park (which bears his mother's family name) and then moved to Ashland. He retired after 41 years in education. He began his career at Westchester High School as a coach and science teacher and then as freshman athletic coach and biology instructor at Springfield High School, where he stayed until appointed principal at Lanphier. Mr. Petefish was our able co-sponsor of Key Club for many years. He said in a retirement article in the Springfield Journal-Register that his greatest accomplishments "have been his continuing fight for four-year high schools, which will return this fall [1968]; and the continuing stable administration and student body close relationship." He was assistant principal at Griffin High School for one or two years and then retired for good. (Mrs. Norton was also there after her retirement from LHS.)

#3 John W. Armitage (6/1968—6/1974: 6 years) was born in Lawrence County, IL and graduated from Illinois State University with a B.S. in Education. He later received an M.S. at the University of Illinois. He was employed by the Springfield School District for 39 years. In those years, he taught and coached at Hay-Edwards Elementary (starting in 1935); then the same at Feitshans High School (1938-1943); taught science at Springfield High and then into administration; his first principalship at Dodds Elementary, followed at Douglas, Hay-Edwards, and Franklin Junior High until he successed Mr. Petefish. He met, however, with stiff yet unsuccessful resistance from the public at his school board approval meeting; 25 vocal parents wanted Herb Scheffler, Mr. Petefish's assistant principal for the previous nine years and his choice for principal. (Scheffler, well liked and with the right counseling touch, was assigned to SHS as principal for a number of years; later, his son, Mark, took the same job.) Mr. Armitage had a 22-year retirement and passed away at age 83.

#4 Phil Schmidt (6/1974—6/1991: 16 years) was a student at Lanphier (class of 1952) where he was a four-year member of the football and track teams and editor of both the *Lan-Hi* and the *Light* (the school newspaper). He graduated from Western Illinois University and then received his M.S. in education from the University of Illinois. He was superintendent of schools in Athens, IL in 1958 before coming into the Springfield school system. Members of his family are also Lanphier alums, including both his brothers, his wife Susan, and his son John. During his long tenure as principal, Mr. Schmidt was known as Lanphier's staunchest supporter and most loyal fan. He was famous for donning his orange sports coat and black trousers for games and other school functions. He was also known for being a tough disciplinarian.

#5 Chuck Flamini (9/1991 – 6/1996: 4 years) was a member of the Lanphier class of 1964. Mr. Flamini attended Eastern Illinois University, where he majored in social studies and competed on the track team. He began his teaching career as an elementary PE teacher. He taught at Wilcox, Ridgely, Sand Hill and Southern View. He was inducted into the Lanphier Hall of Fame in 2003 for his work in education: "Acting Superintendent of Regional Office of Education; Principal of Lanphier High School; Assistant Superintendent of District 186; Curriculum Coordinator of District 186; President of Springfield Education Association; Athletic Director of Lanphier High School." He was principal of SHS and in retirement has been on the School Board, one term as its president.

#6 Larry Rowe (9/1996—6/2005: 8 years) was born in 1951, grew up in Ottawa, IL and attended Western Illinois University, where he received his teaching degree. He student-taught at Lanphier in 1972 and was hired there to teach the following year. He eventually became the guidance counselor at Lanphier. While still the counselor, Mr. Rowe was the coordinator in establishing the Lanphier Hall of Fame. He was appointed principal in the 1996-1997 school year.

#7 Jane Chard (9/2006—6/2008: 2 years) was born and raised in Springfield. After graduating from Springfield High School, she attended Lincoln Land Community College and then received her B.S. from Western Illinois University in education. She later earned her M.A. from Sangamon State University in educational administration. During her career, Jane taught remedial reading, math and English. She was the principal at Douglas School before coming to Lanphier. After her stint at Lanphier she was an administrator in the school district office, where she retired in 2013.

#8 Sheila Boozer (9/2008—12/2010: 2 years) was born in Columbia, MO and raised in Springfield, IL. She attended public schools and graduated from Ursuline Academy. She attended University of Illinois Springfield where she received her B.A. in psychology and Ed.S. in elementary education, and then an M.A. in educational leadership from Eastern Illinois University. Mrs. Boozer taught at Feitshans, Grant and Durfee Magnet in Decatur. She entered the ranks of school administrator as an assistant principal at Graham, then principal at Fairview. She worked in administration at the school district office at 1900 W. Monroe before coming to Lanphier. Mrs. Boozer was next principal at Blackhawk Elementary School and now serves the new superintendent as an administrator in the district office.

#9 Artie Doss (1/2011—Present) is supervising the balance of the three-year grant-based academic remediation plan at Lanphier. He attended Springfield Southeast High School, where he played basketball, football and track. He worked nine years in the coal mines before going to college. He earned an A.A. from Lincoln Land Community College, a B.S. at University of Illinois Springfield and two M.S. Degrees (educational leadership at Eastern Illinois University and reading/literacy at Benedictine University). He taught at all three school levels in District 186 and was assistant principal at Washington Middle School and Douglas Alternative School. Before coming to LHS he was principal of all three alternative education sites here.

Lanphier Alumni Hall of Fame

The recipients each year will be presented with a plaque commemorating their induction into the Hall of Fame and their names will be added to a permanent plaque that is prominently displayed at Lanphier High School. Each inductee must have attended Lanphier for their junior and senior years and graduated at least 25 years before they are nominated. They should have achieved national recognition in their field and serve as an encouragement to current students.

Year	Name	Field
1991	Claude Sowle ('46)	Educator
	William Apblett, Jr. ('39)	Metallurgist
	Donald Baepler ('50)	Educator
	William F. Cellini ('52)	Public Service/ Entrepreneur
	Everett G. Hopson ('63)	Attorney
	William T. Huddleston ('60)	Aerospace Engineer
	Ossie Langfelder ('44)	Public Service
	Robin E. Roberts ('44)	MLB Player/ Hall of Fame
1992	David R. Hammons ('63)	Artist
	Phillip H. Schmidt ('52)	Educator

1993	George E. Schuerman ('41)	Chemist
	Leonard L. Semon ('47)	Educator
1994	Jack A. Siebert, Sr. ('53)	Electrical Engineer
1995	Kathleen Moore Howell ('62)	Humanitarian
1996	Ethel M. Butchek ('67)	Community Activist
1997	Richard L. Jackson ('58)	Microbiologist
	Marry V. Mocnik ('41)	Industrial Relations Consultant
1998	Dean E. Williams ('59)	Photographer
1999	Charles "Chuck" Redpath ('74)	Public Service
2000	Russell Smith ('72)	Movie Producer
2001	Dr. Sean O'Brien ('80)	Chemist
2002	George Colin ('48)	Artist
2003	Charles Flamini ('64)	Educator
2004	Edgar Curtis ('71)	Healthcare Administrator
2005	Alison Novak ('77)	Floral Artist
2006	William R. Dudleston ('76)	Acoustical Engineer
2007	Harold Vose ('55)	Educator
2008	Paul R. Wood ('72)	Investment Analyst
2009	Kevin D. Gamble ('83)	NBA Player

2010	David E. Beatty ('46)	Photographer
	Lt. Col. Jeffrey G. Compton ('86)	Air Force Pilot
2011	Jill R. Grove ('78)	Educator
	Gary W. Willhoit ('65)	Educator
2012	Lawrence Doug Collins ('87)	Coach/Mentor
	Charles Randall Miller ('71)	School Historian
2013	John Marsaglia ('71)	Educator
2014	Dr. Ken Adams ('81)	Physician

Dedications and Themes

Like most annuals, Lanphier's *Lan-Hi* began dedicating each year, usually to a teacher or other staff member. That tradition lasted some 61 years, before switching from a dedication to a theme approach in 1998.

Vol. 1 1936—1937 Robert C. Lanphier   Benefactor

Vol. 2 1937—1938 George E. Stickney   First Principal

Vol. 3 1938—1939 Lee W. Goby   Counselor

Vol. 4 1939—1940 Hulda Albrecht   Soc S./ Counselor

Vol. 5 1940—1941 Nell Plain   *Lan-Hi* Advisor

Vol. 6 1941—1942 "Our Men in the Service"

Vol. 7 1942—1943 "To Those Who Serve"

Vol. 8 1943—1944 J.C. Wetzel   Sci/*Lan-Hi* Advs

Vol. 9 1944—1945 Esther Duncan   Music

Vol. 10 1945—1946 "The Avenue & its Merchants"

Vol. 11 1946—1947 E. Eugene Stevenson Boating Accident

Vol. 12 1947—1948 Freeman C. Goodwin   Distributive Ed

Vol. 13 1948—1949 Edwin E. Sach   Music

Vol. 14 1949—1950 Mabel Kitch   Art

Vol. 15 1950—1951 Atile Chiti   Social Studies

Vol. 16 1951—1952 Students of LHS, Classmates & Friends"

Vol. 17 1952—1953 Emma Parrotte & Mr. Rolla C. Sorrells

Vol. 18 1953—1954 G.E. Stickney   First Principal

Vol. 19 1954—1955 Alice Refine   Mnt Staff

Vol. 20 1955—1956 Frances Chatburn   Math/ Music

Vol. 21 1956—1957 Charles Petefish   Principal

Vol. 22 1957—1958 Mildred Norton   English

Vol. 23 1958—1959 *The Lanphier Light* School paper

Vol. 24 1959—1960 Cleo Dopp   Social Studies

Vol. 25 1960—1961 Ransford, Lober/Matlack   Coaches

Vol. 26 1961—1962 Ethel Furlich   Latin/French

Vol. 27 1962—1963 Orell R. Vanderwater Biology

Vol. 28 1963—1964 Harry Morgan   Printing/Workshop

Vol. 29 1964—1965 Ruth Wineman   Home Economics

Vol. 30 1965—1966 Joe Hoffman   Government

Vol. 31 1966—1967 "Our Generation"

Vol. 32 1967—1968 Inez Gieseking   Yr'book/ Business

Vol. 33 1968—1969 Leonard Semon   Soc.Studies/ NHS

Vol. 34 1969—1970 William Bretz   Govt./History;/S.S.

Vol. 35 1970—1971 Milton Dirst   Chemistry/Physics

Vol. 36 1971—1972 Mary Frances Lavin History

Vol. 37 1972—1973 Nancy Thimus Physical Education

Vol. 38 1973—1974 "Make Your Own Dedication"

Vol. 39 1974—1975 Mr. Armitage / Mr. Schmidt Principals

Vol. 40 1975—1976 Helen Jeske P.E. & Biology

Vol. 41 1976—1977 Lester Brooks Assistant Principal

Vol. 42 1977—1978 Tom Wagner P.E./ Dist. Ed

Vol. 43 1978—1979 Helen Bellamy S.S./School Paper

Vol. 44 1979—1980 J. Barron Robinson Social Science

Robert Thompson Head Custodian

Vol. 45 1980—1981 Mr. & Mrs. Gardner P.E./Wrestl./Eng.

Vol. 46 1981—1982 Lee Halberg Physical Education

Vol. 47 1982—1983 Joe Bonefeste, Ph.D . English

Vol. 48 1983—1984 Robert Nika Driv.Ed/BB Coach

Vol. 49 1984—1985 Leonard Semon Social Science

Ruth Fouts Science

Vol. 50 1985—1986 Georgia Cutsinger Eng./C'leader Adv

Vol. 51 1986—1987 Phil Schmidt Principal

Vol. 52 1987—1988 Ray Bruzan Chemistry/Physics

Vol. 53 1988—1989 Mark Scheffler Mathematics

Vol. 54 1989—1990 Ken Campbell   Math/Computer Sci

Vol. 55 1990—1991 Kristine White   Mathematics

Vol. 56 1991—1992 Nicole Lorton   Senior Dean

Vol. 57 1992—1993 Carol Marcy   Library Assistant

Vol. 58 1993—1994 Charles Flamini   Principal

Vol. 59 1994—1995 Steve Rambach   Social Science

Vol. 60 1995—1996 Deborah Sidener   Business Ed

Vol. 61 1996—1997 Sherry Erickson   Freshman Dean

Vol. 62 1997—1998 "The Fine Points"

Vol. 63 1998—1999 "Out Like a Lion"

Vol. 64 1999—2000 "It's About Time"

Vol. 65 2000—2001 "Are We There Yet?"

Vol. 66 2001—2002 "Lions Have Spirit"

Vol. 67 2002—2003 "Along the Way"

Vol. 68 2003—2004 "ReLION on Each Other"

Vol. 69 2004—2005 "Looks Can Be Deceiving"

Vol. 70 2005—2006 "Visions Become Reality"

Vol. 71 2006—2007 "Northside Story"

Vol. 72 2007—2008 "The Ones to Watch"

Vol. 73 2008—2009 "Every Ending Is a New Beginning"

Vol. 74 2009—2010 "Every Puzzle Takes Time"

Vol. 75 2010—2011 "Make an Uproar"

Vol. 76 2011—2012 "The Secret Life of a Lion"

Vol. 77 2012—2013 "iLion"

Vol. 78 2013—2014 "Jungle Safari"

The Bunn Miracle

J. Bunn Bank and Debts Resulting from 1878 Bank Failure

By Andrew Taylor Call, who placed this article on Wikipedia.com

Jacob Bunn had established a private bank that was called the J. Bunn Bank of Springfield, Illinois. Not to be confused with the Springfield Marine Bank, the J. Bunn Bank rapidly accumulated large capital assets during the nineteenth century, but due to what became an over-extensive portfolio of real estate holdings during the Panic of 1873, the J. Bunn Bank was forced into liquidation.

Jacob Bunn voluntarily effected the liquidation of the bank, and assumed liability for indebtedness that totaled approximately $800,000 in 1878. Jacob Bunn, who acted from deep Christian convictions of honor, honesty, and loyalty, personally assumed liability for the amount of indebtedness that remained after the forced sale of the bank assets failed to produce capital adequate to full satisfaction of the $800,000 debt. The debts were reduced by forced sale of the assets of the J. Bunn Bank to an amount of $572,000.

Consequently, Jacob Bunn, with the assistance of his brother John W. Bunn, and the later assistance of his children, other family members, and numerous close associates and friends, managed to satisfy the remaining 28.5 percent of the original indebtedness. Although Jacob Bunn died in 1897, his children, with the commitment to the fulfillment of their father's desire to repay the entire indebtedness, established a memorial trust that repaid, in 1925, the entire remaining portion of the original debt, a distribution that affected approximately 5,000 persons. The repayment was made with additional interest at the rate of 5 percent per annum.

Author's Note:

When Bob Lanphier III told me about this story of Bunn's accepting responsibility for his bank's failure and insisting that every one of his investors be eventually made whole, I was flabbergasted. Would there be one businessman on Wall Street today who has that kind of honor code?

While this story is a real departure from the story of Lanphier High School and Lanphier's grandfather's role in its existence, I feel this story needed to be told to those, like me, who had never heard it. It is a testament to the integrity of an extraordinary businessman and his family.

It also shines the spotlight on Bunn's younger brother, John W. Bunn, who helped start Sangamo Electric and placed his brother Jacob as its vice president after his bank debacle. It's an added interesting aside that Bunn and Lanphier, the grandsons of two prominent Springfield scions had such a close bond at Sangamo when their grandfathers were ardent supporters of the two candidates in the 1860 presidential race, Bunn for Lincoln and Lanphier for Douglas!

The Enterprising Bunn Brothers

In addition to the Bunns being involved in the formation and running of the Illinois Watch Company and the Sangamo Electric Company, here is a partial list of the brothers' role in the creation of a number of other entrepreneurial enterprises. They spent as much or more time in Chicago in these efforts as in Springfield.

1. Jacob Bunn, John W. Bunn, and many others created and built an honorable system of political promotion and support, networking, and campaign finance support for Abraham Lincoln. This honorable political machine has been referred to by author and Bunn family member, Andrew Taylor Call, as the "Bunn-Lincoln Machine," [See his book, below] the first Republican Party political machine that successfully supported a candidate for the United States Presidency.

2. Jacob Bunn, Abraham Lincoln, and John Todd Stuart served on the railroad committee of the Alton & Springfield Company.

3. John Whitfield Bunn was a long-time president and director of the Springfield Marine Bank.

4. John Whitfield Bunn was co-founder and vice president of the Selz, Schwab Shoe Company of Chicago.

The Selz, Schwab Shoe Company of Chicago was once one of the largest United States shoe and boot manufacturers and possessed nine factories in 1909. The Selz, Schwab Shoe Company employees and their families numbered about 10,000 in 1909.

5. John Whitfield Bunn was a co-founder and director of the Wabash Railroad Company in 1889, a $52 Million corporation in 1889.

6. Jacob Bunn was co-founder and owner of the Chicago Republican Newspaper Company, a $500,000 corporation in 1865.

7. Jacob Bunn was a co-founder of the Chicago & Alton Railroad Company in 1861.

8. Jacob Bunn was a co-founder of the Chicago Secure Depository Company in 1869.

9. John Whitfield Bunn was a co-founder and treasurer of the University of Illinois.

Compiled by Andrew Taylor Call. Citations omitted. See also *Jacob Bunn: Legacy of an Illinois Industrial Pioneer*, Andrew Taylor Call, Brunswick Publishing Corp., Virginia, 2005.

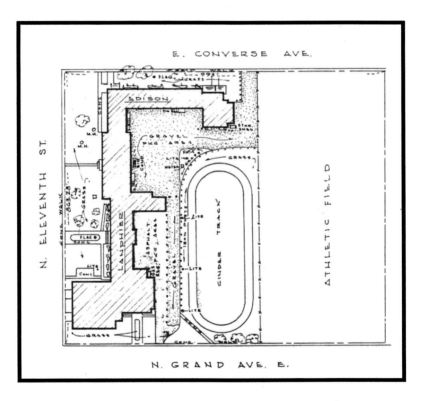

The Lanphier High School campus after the Annex and West Gym addition. 1967 [Courtesy of the Sangamon Valley Collection]

Upgrades to Lanphier High School

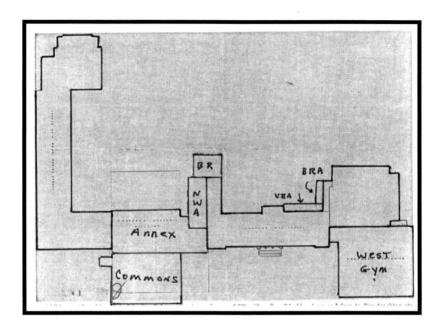

1.   1939   North Wing Addition (NWA)

2.   1948   Band Room (BR

3.   1949   Memorial Stadium

4.   1957   Boiler Room (BRA) and Voc Ed Rooms (VEA) Additions

5.   1969   Annex and West Gymnasium

6.   1998   Commons

Lanphier National Merit® Scholar Finalists

The National Merit® Scholarship program began in 1956. Its mission is to recognize and honor the academically talented high school students across the nation. To be considered, a student must qualify by scoring in the highest percentiles on the PSAT/NMSQT. In 2015 there were 160,000 students who entered, and only 4,700 qualified. From those, 3,100 are Outstanding Participants and their names will be referred to colleges around the country. 1,600 are named as Semi-Finalists, and 1,300 will be Finalists. Eight hundred will be chose from additional criteria to receive a National Achievement Scholarship of $2500.

Those Lanphier students who have been honored as National Merit Finalists have had their pictures and names on the south hall. Here is a list of them.

∞	1976 – 1977	Richard Wood
∞	1978 – 1979	Gregory Augspurger
∞	1978 – 1979	Richard Frank
∞	1981 – 1982	Jacquline Jackson
∞	1982 – 1983	Susan Skufca
∞	1983 – 1984	Edward Green
∞	1986 – 1987	Rebecca Fulk
∞	1986 – 1987	Karen Stutzman
∞	1987 – 1988	Steve Lawrence
∞	1988 – 1989	Christina Munch
∞	1996 – 1997	Dan Craven

Springfield Sports Hall of Fame:
Lanphier Inductees

The Springfield Sports Hall of Fame was started in 1991 by the sports staff at the *Illinois State Journal-Register*. It selects inductees on an annual basis in three categories: Players, Coaches, Team and Friends. See details about their amazing feats at http://www.springfieldsportshalloffame.com/inductees.

The following are those selected from Lanphier High School:

1991	Robin Roberts ('44)	MLB
	Ray Ramsey ('40)	NFL & NBA
	John Schaive ('52)	MLB
	Billy Stone ('43)	NFL
1992	Roger Erickson ('74)	MLB
	Jim Kopatz ('72)	MLB
	Arlyn Lober	Coach
1993	Don Erickson ('57)	MLB
1994	Ron Little ('50)	All-around athlete
1995	Rudy Favero ('43)	MLB
	Vic Antonacci ('55)	Friend
	Ted Boyle	Coach
1996	Allen Crowe ('43)	Auto Racing
1997	Tim Hulett ('78)	MLB
	Rick Schultz ('68)	Standout coll. BB player
1998	Nancy Davenport Derhake ('72)	Prof. Softball player
	Lee Halberg	Coach
	Bob Nika ('55)	S/O LHS athlete/coach
	1983 LHS Basketball	Team
1999	Jim Gardner	Coach

	Mick Madison ('57)	Standout athlete & coll. baseball player
	Rick Lamsargis	Friend
2000	Kevin Gamble ('83)	NBA
	Calvin Petitt ('64)	Standout HS and college BB player
2001	Bob Cain ('45)	Standout HS baseball and BB player
	Ed Horton ('85)	NBA
2003	Bruce Boyle ('55)	Standout HS/college player and coach
2004	George "Bud" Alewelt ('42)	All-around athlete
	Jim Zimmerman ('69)	All-around athlete and coach
2005	Don Hudson ('53)	Standout HS & college in BB/baseball
		1943 LHS Football Team
2008	Ed Ransford	Coach
	Don Post	Player, Coach and Friend
2011	Kevin Jones ('78)	All-around phenomenal athlete
2012	Jennifer Smith ('91)	Standout HS and college athlete
	Gene Strode ('55)	Standout HS/college and coach
	Bruce Edwards ('51)	Friend
2014	Ivan Jackson ('57)	Standout HS and College Basketball player

A Tribute to Ray Ramsey

Ray Ramsey (LHS '40)

The most versatile athlete Springfield has ever produced.

Jim Ruppert, The State Journal-Register *sports editor*

Ray was an extraordinary athlete at Converse and Lanphier High Schools. A Converse High School freshman in 1936-37, he was a multi-sports star--2 years in football and 4 years in basketball and track. The rest of this article is by *Springfield Journal-Register* sports editor Jim Ruppert as a tribute to his friend, on August 26, 2009, upon Ray's passing.

Ray Ramsey, the most versatile athlete Springfield has ever produced, died Tuesday morning at St. John's Hospital after a lengthy illness. He was 88.

The 1940 Lanphier High School graduate was a standout in football, basketball and track. He was one of the original 24 inductees into the Springfield Sports Hall of Fame in 1991; it's one of four Halls of Fame into which Ramsey has been inducted.

He played football and basketball and ran track at Bradley University, winning 13 varsity letters and earning All-America honors or the equivalent in all three. He scored 994 points in basketball, set three school records in track and was a Little All-America halfback in football.

His college career was interrupted by four seasons of military service in the Navy, and when he came back he captained a Bradley basketball team that went 25-7. He also beat the world record-holder, Earl Dugger, in the 120-yard high hurdles at the Boston AAU meet. Ramsey once logged 27 consecutive first-place track and field finishes at Bradley — while competing in five different events. He also held school records in both hurdles events and the high jump and later served four years as Bradley's track coach.

After his senior year at Bradley in 1947, he played in the College All-Star football game at Soldier Field, and the All-Stars scored one of their rare wins over the pros, a 16-0 decision over the Chicago Bears. Two of his teammates were Buddy Young and Elroy "Crazy Legs" Hirsch.

Ramsey played 10 seasons of professional football in three different leagues and was an All-Pro flanker while playing for Hamilton in the Canadian Football League. He spent two seasons in the NBA with the Tri-City Blackhawks and Baltimore Bullets, but by then the two-sport grind was too much.

In football, he played for the Chicago Cardinals in the NFL from 1950-53, and in his final season with the team he intercepted 10 passes and returned them a team-record 237 yards.

In a 1991 interview, Ramsey said his favorite sport was the one he was playing.

"It was such a great thing to participate at that level," Ramsey said. "They were all my favorite. It depended on what season it was."

He played until he was 37 before returning to Bradley and coaching the track team for four years while he was playing pro football.

Ramsey was hired as teacher at Lanphier in 1958 and served as head track coach and assistant basketball and football coach. He spent almost 30 years teaching at his alma mater, retiring in 1986. In the summers, he also ran a summer track program that featured, among others, his daughters and Kim Schofield Werth.

"I spent more time with him from age 15 to 27 than I did with anybody," said Kim Werth, also a charter member of the Springfield Sports Hall of Fame and an eight-time individual state track champion while at Southeast. "We had a great friendship, a great respect for one another. I loved the man."

Those Awesome Gardner Boys

1. **Frank Gardner** ('83) – 52-21, 25 falls

    at SE his freshman year

2. **Jeff Gardner** (would have grad. in '85) – 68-7,

    26 falls in 2 years

    > MV Freshman '82
    >
    > MV Sophomore '83
    >
    > MV Wrestler '82 & '83
    >
    > Tournaments won
    >
    > City – '82 &'83
    >
    > Conference– '82 & '83
    >
    > Morton–'83
    >
    > Quincy– '82 & '83
    >
    > Lincoln– '82 & '83
    >
    > Regional– '82 & '83
    >
    > Sectional– '83-3rd
    >
    > State Place –'83-6th

3. **Mike Gardner** ('86) – 134-21, 55 falls

    > MV Freshman- '83
    >
    > MV Sophomore-'83
    >
    > MV Wrestler- '86
    >
    > Tournaments won
    >
    > City—'83, '84, '85, '86
    >
    > Conference--'85, '86
    >
    > Morton—'86

Lincoln—'84, '85, '86

Regional—'84, '85, '86

Sectional – '84-3rd; '85- 3rd; '86-2nd

4. Andrew Gardner 1'89) – 151-8, 85 falls

MV Freshman-'86

MV Sophomore- '87

MV Wrestler- '86, '87, '88, '89

Tournaments won

City – '86, '87, '88, '89

Conference-'86, '87, '88, '89

Morton—'87, '88, '89

Quincy—'86, '87, '88,'89

Lincoln—'86, '89

Regional—'86, '87, '88,'89

Sectional—'86 -3rd; '87-1st; '88-1st; '89-1st

State Place—'87-3$^{rd;}$ **'88-1st**; '89-2nd

Summary: Gardner Stats from '80-'89 Totals

405-57

191 falls

46 tournament championships

GOLD STARS

In Commemoration of Those Lanphier High School Students and Alumni Who Made the Supreme Sacrifice in Our Country's Service

World War II

Frank D. Baliva

Thomas Roberts

Fred Bourgasser

Robert Sallade

Charles Cardoni

Leonard Schroll

David D. Drone

George Sneckus

Heinz Koblalka

B.S. Stillwagon

Raymond Lehnen

Elbert Stratton

Paul Norris

George Veneri

John Peacher

Joseph Weedman

Louis Pickett

Henry Yonk

Korean War

Viet Nam War

L.Cpl. Glen E. King

Persian Gulf War

Afganistan War

Iraq War

Please let us know if there are other Lanphier relatives or friends, in addition to the above heroes, who had given their lives in these wars or other events in the service of our country. Thank you.

Speech to the National Honor Society Initiation Ceremony Lanphier High School on April 5, 1966

Charliene Tucker Kloppenburg (Class of 1945)

It is truly an honor to be here today and have a part in this ceremony. Many noble thoughts are brought to mind in considering the four distinguished qualities upheld here: Scholarship, Leadership, Service, and Character.

Wouldn't you say that Character is the most personal of all these traits? We could not aspire to excel in the other three without good character…and it is true we cannot have high ideals unless we are taught by loving parents and dedicated teachers….Yet the character we possess is our own making. God has given each of us an inborn conscience to know right from wrong.

My 8th grade teacher from Bunn School, Laura Kiser, made certain that not a student passed through her classes without learning these words from the poet Robert Burns: "An honest man, though ere so poor, is King of men for-a that."

This challenge to live your life in honesty, in purity, with humility and courtesy towards others is a challenge you accept while you are young. You begin now, bit by bit every day of your life you will be called upon to make righteous decisions. A good character is built upon daily trials. The cost of Liberty is Vigilance. So it is with a strong character;

and the price of any sort of excellence is self-discipline. Day by day we build our character 'til we become what we ARE. Maurice Chevalier was recently quoted in our Sunday *Newsweek* magazine as saying: "When you are 20, you have the face God gave you; at 40 you have the face you made yourself; and at 60 you have the face you deserve."

It is wise to know where we are going, what we hope to become—so we'll like the face we see in the mirror—so that our inner beauty will light the hopes of others.

Think with me now and see what Character can do to the other three virtues honored here. Character added to Scholarship promotes INTEGRITY; added to Leadership it gives DIRECTION; and to service it brings DEDICATION AND LOYALTY. All of this adds up to JOY and a zest for living, a REVERENCE for life!

Build yourself a noble Character and never forget the high ideals you aspire to today!

Note written on the bottom of the speech by Charliene: *Miss Furlich* [the long-time Latin teacher who was also the long-time National Honor Society advisor] *asked me to come to be one of the speakers 21 years after* [my own] *graduation.*

A Boy's Park:
A Trip through Reservoir Park around 1925

By Howard Hoehn,* June 25, 2014 [Rev. July 26, 2014]

Like most all North-End kids, I played in Reservoir Park during my youth. I moved from East Converse in 1924 at the age of eight to 1112 North Grand Avenue East, just across the street, south of the park. I can't remember a day during my first years there that I didn't run over to the park whenever I could get away. I so loved that park that I want to write down what it was like, best I can at the ripe ole age of 97. I want people to know what it looked like. Even though that park is long gone (torn down in 1933), perhaps talking about it will stir future generations to have some virtual idea of what I experienced and what they will have missed. Who knows, maybe someday a rich person with a heart and love of the past will duplicate the park in some nearby setting so kids will appreciate it as much as my friends and I did.

The 24-acre park was bounded on the south by East North Grand Ave, on the north by Converse Ave., on the west by North 11th St., and on the east by Michigan Avenue. The park included the big reservoir, the lagoon, a dry hollow that once was a second lagoon, children's playground, the Pavilion, tennis courts and the baseball park. It was surrounded on all sides by two rows of large cottonwood trees, some of which survived the park's destruction.

The reservoir itself was some 30 feet deep and its steep inner sides were lined with slabs of stone, and there was a ledge going around the rectangular top. It had a steel fence on the inside of the ledge which acted as a sidewalk for people to walk completely around it and yet not fear falling in. In the very center was a stone pier that stood about six feet above the water line. A fluted pipe extended out in the middle of the pier and had an elaborate statue arrangement consisting of soldiers, horses, weapons and such that appeared to be made of wrought iron and painted black. The resulting fountain spewed out water during the summer months, adding to the beauty and importance of the reservoir. It was a sight to behold, at least in my young mind.

You'd hear stories about people drowning in the reservoir. The one that I can personally verify happened when I was a kid. A lady who lived next door—I don't want to give any names—had a son who lived by the railroad tracks on 13th Street. He had three sons and two daughters. One day he goes over and climbs up to the reservoir, jumps the fence and ties a cord around his neck and dove in. The note he left said, "You'll find me at the end of the cord." Figure that out: why a person with a family would kill himself.

You could climb up onto the top of the reservoir on a set of 41 steps on the middle of its north face—that is, unless you wanted to scale any of the sides which we kids did regularly. At ground level on either side of the staircase were a light standard and bases for handrails. About half-way up and at the top there were two more sets of concrete bases for the railings. On the west side of the reservoir, at ground level and right in the center, stood an imposing wall of stone about six-feet in height and two feet thick and on top of it sat a commemorative plaque designating the reservoir as the city's water supply in the 1800s. Near that "wall" was a concrete and iron slab for access to the controls for the reservoir. There were a number of bushes planted on the sloping side of the reservoir behind the wall. There were also lots of bushes placed about half-way up in the center of the south slope.

Another central feature of the park was the lagoon which ran east and west on the north end of the park, probably three blocks long and four and a half-feet deep. It stretched all the way from the west slope of the reservoir to the west side of the ballpark. It had a concrete retaining wall on its west end that turned a right angle and extended another 15 feet or so on the south, where a boat was parked; the rest of the lagoon had a natural border with the grass. There were two islands in the lagoon, the one on the west was elongated and the one on the east side was round and not very large— maybe 10 feet in diameter. The lagoon narrowed in the middle forming a neck.

There was a depression on the very west side of the park, next to 11th Street, that I heard used to be filled with water forming another figure-eight lagoon. When I was a child, it was dry and called the "Hollow," running about two blocks and the same depth as the lagoon—four or four and a half-feet. A large playground was located just to the east of the hollow and south of the Pavilion. It consisted of an assortment of games and equipment, such as a very large sand box with a two-way slide within, some large metal pieces that were remnants of a large swing. Just outside of the sandbox stood a merry-go-round, a teeter-totter and a swing set. There was a drinking fountain there too.

The only building in the park (aside from the baseball stadium) was the Pavilion, which was sandwiched between the north end of the reservoir and the Dry Hollow. The large white frame building served as a concession in the summer time and a place to sit down and put your ice skates on in the winter. The basement housed the men's (north end) and ladies'(south end) restrooms, and the middle section had the park office and storage room. (When the reservoir was being demolished later the pavilion was used to store the WPA workers' tools.)

The park superintendent was Conrad "Conn" Noll, granddaddy of the present-day Noll attorneys. Conn had one or two employees working for him. He would have them walk around the park, with gunny sacks hanging from a rope around their shoulders, picking up scraps of paper, etc. (using a broomstick handle with a nail on the end), keeping the park clean.

The security guard was John "Doc" Hargreave. He was probably in his seventies and had a big handlebar mustache. Ole Doc had a hearing problem so that if you met up with him and said, "Hi, Doc," you usually got an answer of "Oh, about…" and he'd pull out his gold-chained watch and check the time and give it to you. Occasionally he'd offer me a nickel to go over and take down the tennis court nets. Doc's best time of day was 9:00 p.m.—that's when he made it a point to be at the southwest corner of the reservoir and blow his whistle and yell "It's nine o'clock and out you go!" Our hangout was at that same corner under a large tulip tree so we kids would go out of the park but sneak back around the east side of the reservoir and climb up to the top and aggravate him. He'd come over there and say "Come

337 - North-End Pride

down off that hill or I'll burn the shirts right off your backs!"
He actually carried a gun and fired it once in a while, but up
in the air.

That park was a second home to me and it gave a lot
of enjoyment to me and lots of other people—young,
medium and old. Churches and other organizations had ice
cream socials in it, held just south of the playground near the
Hollow. Children got enjoyment from the playground. And
ice skaters enjoyed the lagoon in winter; sledders got their
kicks on the slopes of the reservoir. During the contentious
coal wars in Illinois, miners would hold some of their union
meetings in front of the wall.

There of course was lots to do in that park when the
weather was nice. There was an organized program for boys
and girls when school was out: teenagers enjoyed
woodworks, sewing and volleyball, as well as softball. Then,
in the evenings they had softball programs for the young
men, some at the ballpark, or behind it and to the west of it.
That lagoon got its share of fishermen in the summer too.
When they would let excess water out of the reservoir, the
water would be directed into the lagoon from a drain tile on
the northeast corner. Where the overflow drain pipe from the
reservoir entered the lagoon was a place where the crappie
would be biting.

The unemployed—especially during the Depression
years—took advantage and enjoyed the park. Some played
Rummy—four hands for a nickel. Blackjack was a favorite
game and was played for kitchen matches. (Steinkuhlers and
Nolls' Grocery sold them for a nickel a box.). Then there was
horseshoes to play in the hollow for many of the men.

The Pavilion's concession stand sold candy, ice cream, soda, peanuts, popcorn, etc. The candy caramels cost two for a penny. A long licorice stick or a jaw breaker cost a penny. A frozen candy bar—Milkyway, Snicker, Baby Ruth and O'Henry—each sold for a nickel.

I don't know if they sold tobacco or not, but here's what that stuff cost back then. The price of a package of cigarettes, such as Camels, Luckies, Chesterfields, and Old Golds, was 15¢; Wings and Marvels cost 10¢. For the chewers, BeechNut, Red Man, Star and Horse Shoe sold for 10¢; Browns Mule and Spark Plug for a nickel. If you rolled your own cigarettes, Bull Durham cost 10¢; but Golden Grain could be had for a nickel.

The concession was closed for the winter, but was used for ice skaters to change from shoes to skates and a place to get warm after skating and sledding.

The baseball stadium you see there today opened new on May 13, 1925. (Before that there was just a simple baseball diamond with a ramshackle set of bleachers.) The Springfield team was the Senators, backed by the Washington Senators and a member of the Three-I League, class B. We lost that first game but it didn't dampen the spirits of the fans. There were so many people who came out that Wednesday afternoon that the bleachers were packed and fans crowded along the outside of both baselines. That team thrived and had good attendance until the Depression hit. It's been rough here in town for professional teams ever since.

Some years the ballpark was used for Muni League baseball and softball as well. Boxing and wrestling shows have been held there as well as donkey baseball, baseball and barn-storming teams and major league players. High school football, baseball, and track meets were also held there before Memorial Stadium was built in 1949.

Reservoir Park was full of trees everywhere you looked—hundreds of 'em. The big majority were American Elms. Close to our hangout, as I mentioned, a tall, straight tulip tree grew and south of the stadium clubhouse there was a catalpa tree—what we called cigar trees. There were also a few soft maples growing in the playground and pavilion area.

There were flower beds lining all along North Grand and Converse. In the fall they allowed the neighbors to dig up and take home geranium and canna bulbs for next spring's planting. They were a sight to see, I can tell you--beautiful.

All and all, Reservoir Park was one nice place and a big benefit to many for a lot of years. If they needed to build a school, two blocks north would have suited the purpose: the Old Circus Grounds between Watch and Black Avenues. Directly across the street was railroad property that has been for sale since I was a kid and that's a lot of years. That property will now be used for the Railroad Relocation—another upcoming snafu…politics!

We also used the park for shooting off fireworks. During the Depression a cheap firecracker for the Fourth of July was a Karo Syrup or a Cocoa can with a pressed in lid and a hole punched in the bottom. Add a little carbide and water, put the can on the ground, hold it down with your foot, put a lighted match to the hole and BANG. Now go fetch the lid and start over again.

Baseball

I have to digress a bit here and talk about some stories in connection with that ball park and baseball. I lived for baseball and played it into adulthood. (Later I took up softball.) First, I was a pretty fair ball player and one day, just fooling around, I stood at the first base line and threw a baseball all the way over the left field fence—probably 320 feet. Woodrow Wilson Emmons was my witness. Another time there was a boxing match at night in the stadium. There was this white boy fighting this colored boy and the white boy was getting clobbered and the fans were on the colored boy's side. Some man who ran a grocery story on Peoria Road hollered out, "N_____ lovers!" He was shouted down and the crowd made him leave.

My final story is about the baseball team I was on the summer of '40. The Clover Farm team was good enough to make it to Rockford where we won. [Howard was on loan from another team— see below for his summary of his amateur baseball career.] From there we went to a South Side ballpark in Chicago (not Comiskey Park) and got beat. We played the next game in Wrigley Field where I played center field. What a team we had. I still have the last ball from the Rockford Amateur Tournament signed by my teammates and me.

My Time in Muni Baseball

I started playing softball in 1936 (age 19) and didn't start playing hardball until 1939 (at age 21). In 1940, I was playing for Honrahan & Wattling in Springfield's Muni League. Our competitor, Clover Farm, won the tournament for this district and advanced to the next level at Rockford. They were allowed to pick up a couple additional players and they chose me as one of them.

We won the Rockford Tournament and advanced to Chicago, where we played the winner of the Chicago district. We played at a South Side park on a Saturday afternoon and got beat. On Sunday we played the same team, the Chicago Yanks, and again got beat, 4-3. The winner got to go to Battle Creek, Michigan, to play in the Amateur World Series.

In 1946—the first year back from the armed forces—Andy O'Neill and Stan Patrick had the [Paul] Weidenbacher team already picked. We won 49 games and lost one, late in the season. We accomplished this with only eight position players and three pitchers, four of us also played softball for Rosies-Rhule Busy Summer—sometimes a double-header, evening and night. In addition, we all also had day jobs.

Andy O'Neill, left, and Howard Hoehn

[Courtesy Illinois State Journal-Register]

*Howard Hoehn, *born in 1917, still has an excellent memory and plenty of stories at 97, as you can tell from this article he wrote. (When I gave the manuscript back to him all typed up, he made several corrections I missed.) He is one of the last Rabbit Row residents alive who has a detailed knowledge of Reservoir Park and what it looked like. He attended Converse Grade School and continued there for his freshman year of high school. He then went to Springfield High where he graduated with the January 1936 class (along with a boyhood friend, my uncle & local artist, Marshall Mitchell).*

He worked in Springfield his whole life and lived most of it on South 13th, with his wife of 68 years, Mary. He and Mary now live in a retirement home in town. His hobbies include following the Cubs and making pictures and models. He was one of the two men who made a model of Reservoir Park. (He recently gave me the model, which I plan on donating to Lanphier High School, along with the 1940 Clover Farm baseball autographed by the entire team, hopefully for a small archives in the LHS library, along with other memorabilia.)

Howard's employment arc spanned several careers: grocer and baker (4 years); factory worker (2 years); Army clerk (4 years); construction worker (4-½ years); plumbing and heating construction, office manager and accountant (17 years); State Department of Rehab, accountant (1-½ years); State DOT, accountant (8-½ years); plus "some small-time jobs not included."

Edward Oliver Lanphier Prizes in Mathematics and Science

Edward Oliver Lanphier was born August 10, 1902 in Springfield, IL, the son and first child of Robert Carr Lanphier, Sr. and Bertha Oliver Lanphier. He attended Springfield High School for his freshman and half of his sophomore years. He went to the Choate School in Wallingford, CT in January of 1917 and graduated in June of 1919.

That September of 1919, he entered Yale University in New Haven, CT and studied in the Sheffield Scientific School for a degree in Electrical Engineering. Both at Choate and at Yale he was an outstanding student.

While at Yale, he developed a strep infection and returned to Springfield for treatment. Unfortunately, without sulfur or penicillin, he was not able to recover and passed away at home on the 22nd day of September 1922, at the beginning of his senior year.

In 1922, his parents established two prizes in Edward's name, one at Yale for the outstanding student studying in the Department of Electrical Engineering, and two prizes at Springfield High School—Mr. Lanphier's alma mater— one prize for those students excelling in Mathematics and the second prize for those students excelling in Science. Each prize had a Winner and an Honorable Mention, a total of four awards were to be given at SHS each year.

The prizes at Springfield High School were funded annually by Edward's parents and, after the death of R.C. Lanphier, Sr., by Edward's mother, Bertha, until the late 1950s. At that time Robert C. Lanphier, Jr., Edward's

Brother, funded the prizes for several years until 1960. When he was out of town, the Springfield School District asked his son, Robert "Bob" C. Lanphier III to fund them, and he has since that date.

In 1984, Bob Lanphier extended the Edward Oliver Lanphier Prizes in Mathematics and Science to the other two public high schools in Springfield, Lanphier High School and Feitshans High School (now Springfield Southeast High School). These prizes have been awarded at all three of these high schools ever since.

Originally cash prizes, the awards after 1965 consisted of both cash and the standard scientific reference book, the hefty *CRC Handbook of Chemistry and Physics*. When that book was obsoleted in 2010 by all its reference information being online, one or two current science books took its place, such as *Dealers of Lightning - Xerox PARC and the Dawn of the Computer Age* by Michael A. Hiltzik and *The Singularity Is Near* by Ray Kurzweil. In 2013, the prizes were once again only cash. That year the awardees received $300.00 for the Winner and the $150.00 for Honorable Mention for each prize at each of the three schools.

The display of Lanphier's Earth Day flag was presented by chemistry teacher Ray Bruzan to The National Museum of American History of the Smithsonian Institution, in Washington, D.C. It was placed in this permanent display on November 8, 1994. [Courtesy of Ray Bruzan]

Author's Note

In the Preface I shared with you that this book began as a small history insert into my personal experiences at Lanphier, my memoir I was writing for my 50th Class Reunion. I had finished that rough draft of *Happy Times at Lanphier High: Memoir of the Class of '62*—the working title—and put it away.

My plan is to rework, polish, and then publish it next year. It won't be a sequel to this book, but a stand-alone honest memoir of my adolescent years, embarrassing as they sometimes are, set at Edison Junior High and then the three years at Lanphier Senior High.

If any of my classmates would like to contribute their personal experiences or observations about that time in your lives, please contact me. That invitation is extended to all those Lanphier alums who were in school around the time I was, between 1958 and 1962.

You may contact me through my publishing company address on the copyright page or at my website, www.kenmitchellbooks.com.

I am also planning to write a book on the lives and episodes of North-End men and women, and their families. If any of you would like to contribute to *North-End Memories*, please contact me. You can either identify yourself in the book or remain anonymous. Your stories can include things that happened while working at one of the North-End factories or businesses, growing up in your neighborhoods, being a student at Lanphier or a grade school, etc.

About the Author

Ken Mitchell is a local author who has written three other books and several shorter pieces. He has degrees from Millikin University in history and political science and Sangamon State University in biology and education.

He has had an enjoyable and varied 40-year career, starting and running several businesses, including real estate, farming, horse breeding, and insurance. He was also a commodities broker, corporate recruiter and trainer. He ended his business career in sales and marketing.

Among his interests are flying (he's a licensed pilot), sports cars, world religions, reading, and tennis.

Ken has five children: Robb, an U.S. Army Lieutenant Colonel (wife Sue); Todd, also an U.S. Army Lieutenant Colonel (wife Tracy); Brett, in food services; Ladd, in the music industry (wife Emily); and Zemfira, a senior in high school.

Ken and his wife, Karen Kelly, a retired elementary teacher, live in Springfield, IL. They have five grandchildren: Brody, Tegan, Simon, Calliope and Audree. Ken and Karen enjoy traveling, especially in and around the San Juan Mountains in Southwest Colorado.

Ken, a past member of the National Speakers Association, is a Certified Toastmaster. As a public speaker and trainer, Ken puts on seminars on writing family histories and memoirs. He is also available for group speaking through his website, www.kenmitchellbooks.com.

Seagull Press will donate a portion of the profits from this book to assist author and minister, Wayne Muller, in his charity work, Bread for the Journey.

> Its Mission: To find people with strength and vision who are passionate about improving their community, and help them make it happen.

> Its Vision: To nurture the seed of generosity that exists in every human heart.

For a description of this work, go to breadforthejourney.org. If you're interesting in starting a local chapter, contact the charity directly.

I wholeheartedly recommend Muller's best-selling book *How Then, Shall We Live?: Four Simple Questions That Reveal the Beauty and Meaning of Our Lives*. In it he poses and then answers these four profound questions in a wonderful narrative:

Who am I?
What do I love?
How shall I live, knowing I will die?
What is my gift to the family of the earth?

To Order Quickly

Call 217-787-7100

When leaving a message do not give credit card information

Or

Go to our Website at

kenmitchellbooks.com

PayPal or Major Credit Cards accepted